GLORY *to* GLORY

GLORY to GLORY

*Personal Meditations
for the New Millennium*

Sr. Francis Clare, SSND

Resurrection Press
Mineola • New York

Acknowledgements

IN A VERY SPECIAL WAY, I want to thank everyone who supported me in the writing of this book: prayer warriors, discerners, intercessors. May God reward each and every one of you as only God can.

I especially want to acknowledge and thank Betty Kayser for her priceless service in spending countless hours of her time in the initial typing and subsequent revisions of the manuscript.

Thank you, too, to all who have been part of my life and allowed me to see Jesus through them and to experience the God of glory: the Sisters and family I have lived with, the students I have taught, the countless others I have come to know as friends and have been privileged to minister to in teaching, in prayer, and in healing love.

First published in 1998 by Resurrection Press, Ltd.
P.O. Box 248, Williston Park, NY 11596

Copyright © 1998 by Sr. Francis Clare, S.S.N.D.

ISBN 1-878718-46-0
Library of Congress Catalog Card Number 97-75615

All Scriptures are from New International Version (NIV) unless otherwise indicated.

	New Jerusalem Bible	NJB
	New American Bible	NAB
	New Revised Standard Version	NRS
	New International Version	NIV
	Revised English Bible	REB
	An Inclusive Version	AIV

Cover design by John Murello.

Printed in the United States of America.

Contents

Prayer Before Reading

TEACH ME, O GOD, by Your Holy Spirit what it means to quiet my mind, to pray from my heart, to allow my whole being to become restful before You.

Unlock that special part of my heart where I feel love, compassion, and trust—where no one else is allowed but You, O God. You alone have the key to that place that cannot be touched, influenced or moved by anything except Your grace and Your presence.

This is a time for my mind to listen and my heart to respond. It is a time for You, O God, to whisper to my heart what it is that You want me to hear. Help me to be patient, quiet, listening, so that what You have spoken in my heart I may hear You whisper in my mind.

O God, more than anything else, as I move through this book, allow me to move quickly from thinking to praying, from thought to prayer.

Amen!

You are encouraged to write your own reflection or prayer after each day's reading experience.

Preface

BACK IN MY EARLY DAYS of the Charismatic Renewal, when I first met Sister Fran, I questioned, "Why is she so excited about God?"

After reading *Wow, God* and then *Your Move, God*, I, too, became excited about God's love and power working in, with and through us today.

Here was a daughter of the Father who did not apologize for how God powerfully touched her life, or, apologize for her use of the gifts of the Spirit which she rapidly matured in. Also, I realized that Jesus Christ was an absolute reality and love in her life.

When *We, the Bride* was completed and Sister Fran said, "That's it!", my sense was a resounding "No!" Why? Because Jesus, the Bridegroom prepares His Bride to be brought into the glory of the Father. Thus, *Glory to Glory* would become the most important book as we all look forward to entering into the final glory of our Father's House.

Because of Sister Fran's obedience, all who read this devotional will be drawn closer to and deeper into the Father's glorious love and presence.

Thank you, Sister Fran, for your "Yes" to writing this book.

DR. BERNIE KLAMECKI

Introduction

"IT IS ALL IN THE Pantry of My Divine Stillness. Every word, every understanding, every phrase. You come and get it."

This prophetic promise was given to me in 1992 as I stood in the waters of the Jordan, as our Israel Pilgrimage group prayed over me for blessing on a new book that God had just begun to speak to me about.

Before leaving Milwaukee, enroute to the Chicago O'Hare Airport, the word came in prayer with Dr. Bernie Klamecki, "Sister Fran, the Lord would say to you that there is another book in you and you are to claim the anointing for it in the Holy Land."

I gasped and sputtered, "But I have announced to the world that *We, the Bride* is my 'Swan Song'. How could I be writing another book?"

On pilgrimage from September 29 to October 7, every time our group prayed for an anointing in places like Nazareth, Cana, Tabor, Calvary, Mt. Zion, they would see the glory come down. I could not deny that God was confirming that there was another book in me. Prophecies, visions, words kept affirming the call to write. A constant flow of glory Scriptures from the Old and New Testament came forth—words like:

"In the morning you will see the glory of the Lord" (Ex 16:7).

"They will see the glory of the Lord, the splendor of our God" (Is 35:2).

"And the glory of the Lord will be revealed, and all mankind together will see it; for the mouth of the Lord has spoken" (Is 40:5).

1992 was my tenth year to lead all the prayer services for a Holy Land Pilgrimage. The highlight was to take part in the Christian Celebration of the Jewish Feast of the Tabernacles. Out of the entire Celebration, with all of its learned, convicting and convincing teachings, this statement alone stood out: "Once the glory is released there will be no other theme until He comes in glory."

In one golden moment, as if announced by a trumpet blast I knew that the title for the book was *Glory to Glory.* Like Dr.

Bernie, I had the sense it was to be more than just a book. It would be "God's manual for revival and survival." "No other theme until He comes in glory!" A glory book! *Glory to Glory!* God would give it, I would receive it.

On returning home, I scrawled "Glory to Glory" across the entire month of August 1993 in my Five-Year Planner. With awe I watched God miraculously provide a cottage on the North Shore of Oahu to be "the Pantry of His Divine Stillness" where I might receive "every word, every understanding, every phrase."

The Lord's direction for a disciplined stay was for me to look up the word "Glory" in Strong's Concordance. To my amazement, there were more than four hundred "glory" references from both the Old and New Testaments!

Together with several Bibles, these Glory Scriptures were all I needed for my thirty-day stay in God's Pantry. They were my key and my discipline to hear from God for thirty days and thirty nights. I felt like Moses being called to the top of Mt. Sinai. "And the glory of the Lord settled on Mount Sinai. For six days the cloud covered the mountain, and on the seventh day the Lord called to Moses from within the cloud" (Ex 24:16).

On August 1, I boarded United Flight 290 and claimed Seat 19F. The present of God's presence was waiting for me. I knew that God was there ready to do everything that needed to be done. More than anything else I was called to sit back, to let go, and to enjoy the present of His presence.

"Enter into My presence. Stay in My presence. Bask in My presence. I am here for you every step of the journey. You can trust Me, your God."

In flight, I jotted in my journal what God continued to speak. "This is not something you are programming. I am the Master Planner, the Omniscient Designer, and the Omnipotent Worker. Allow Me to do what has been in My heart and My mind from all eternity." If I had any doubts about what God was doing or what I was called to do, Jesus now seemed to be saying to me: "Power will not be lacking to you for the work I call you to do."

The glory of the Lord filled the plane where I was sitting and everyone in it, whether they were aware of it or not. As I looked out the window, I saw with eyes of faith the magnificence of those clouds in glory. "At that time the sign of the Son of Man will appear in the sky, and all the nations of the earth will mourn.

They will see the Son of Man coming on the clouds of the sky, with power and great glory" (Mt 24:30).

By the time we neared Honolulu, the glory of the night had settled over the city. God's voice was reassuring: "As you have asked, I have flooded this place with My glory. Indeed My glory is upon this place. It is just a beginning. I will speak the word that I would have My people hear.

"I will not be silent. I will speak to you in the beauty of this place, the majesty of the waters, the course of the winds, the elegance of the foliage and the flowers.

"I will move in the power of My Spirit for a world that needs My Spirit. Indeed this is My plan and I thank you for being part of it. Nothing, absolutely nothing, shall thwart My work. I have sent a legion of angels to minister to you and to protect you from all Powers of Darkness. Victory is Mine! Glory is Mine! My glory shall go forth from this place to the ends of the earth!"

All this God wanted me to hear before I deplaned about 9:30 p.m.

So that I "lacked for no good thing," the Lord provided me shepherds in the flesh, Francis and Hazel Kennedy, Honolulu's leaders in the Catholic Charismatic Renewal.

Over and over that night I prayed the Moses' prayer in Exodus 33:18: "Lord, show me Your glory." Over and over I would wake with the sense of the Shekinah Glory—God's visible manifestation of majesty in power, which once filled the Tabernacle (Ex 40:34)—being on this place and flooding both my room and my heart! As if that were not enough, God's further words that night were: "And in the morning you will see the glory of the Lord" (Ex 16:7).

In my dream world I responded: "Yes Lord! Yes! Here! Now! Your Glory!"

Morning came and so did an ever deepening awareness of God's presence. All the beauty I had read and heard about was right outside my window. The ride across the mainland to the North Shore, Laie, with its extravaganza of lush foliated mountainsides was spectacular! My heart sang out "I lift my eyes toward the mountains whence shall help come to me? . . . The Lord will guard your coming and your going both now and forever" (Ps 121:8).

Not only did God's angels accompany us from the mainland to the North Shore, but on arriving at 55347 Kamehameha, I knew that God had sent angels ahead to tidy up my "prayer pantry" and to bring down an anointing of His glory.

Knowing what great things God had done and was ready to do, I sang forth Mary's Canticle: "My being proclaims the greatness of the Lord, my spirit finds joy in God my Savior, for he has looked upon his servant in her lowliness. . . . God who is mighty has done great things for me, holy is his name; his mercy is from age to age on those who fear him" (Lk 1:46-50).

There was no doubt in my mind that this "age to age" mercy would be here in abounding measure day by day.

Here I would bask in the steadfast love of the Lord that never ceases and trust in His mercies that never come to an end. Every morning His mercies would be new for me. Here I would live in God's Holy Presence, seek His face, listen for His voice, bask in His glory, for thirty days and thirty nights.

God, take me into the Pantry of Your Divine Stillness. Speak to my heart. I am listening. I desire to receive from You the revelation of Your glory. I need Your miracle power, O God, to stay in Your presence, one task, one day at a time. You have said: "The book is in My presence." My life is in Your presence.

But I keep weaving in and out of that presence. My left brain would take me many places in search of ways to help You out, O God, on paths where You are not leading. You are saying to me today, "It is all in My presence. Here, I will lead. Here, I will deliver. Here you can trust Me for your next direction. I will not fail you."

Father, Son, and Holy Spirit, I lift up into Your magnanimous heart all whom You are calling to share this devotional. It is Your book. It is Your Word that needs to go forth to Your people so that all may receive the revelation of Your glory. Lift us up right now above all that is doom and gloom in our lives. Flood us with Your power! Flood us with Your glory!

Let Your anointing fall! As Your glory filled the temple, flood our temples with Your glory.

1

GLORY OF YOUR PRESENCE

Blessed are those who have learned to acclaim you, who walk in the light of your presence, O Lord. They rejoice in your name all day long; they exult in your righteousness. For you are their glory and strength, and by your favor you exalt our horn.

(Ps 89:15-17)

FROM THE MOMENT WE ARRIVED God centered my attention on His presence above everything else! Whatever else was or was not there—His Divine Presence was there!

The all-holy God was present in this place which would become my Nazareth, my Galilee, my Tabor, my Jerusalem!

As in Nazareth, God would find a dwelling place among the pots and pans of a simple kitchen, an unpretentious workspace and this off-the-oceanfront lounge and bedroom. As in Galilee, I would see Him walking on the waters. As on Tabor, I would see Him in glory in the heights of Laie. As in Jerusalem, I would come to ponder and to know the glory of the Word made flesh and come to dwell among us.

"The Lord has established his throne in heaven, and his kingdom rules over all. Bless the Lord, all you his angels, you mighty in strength, who do his bidding, obeying his spoken word" (Ps 103:19-20) (NRS).

"You are clothed with majesty and glory, robed in light as with a cloak. You spread out the heavens like a tent; you raised your palace upon the waters. You make the clouds your chariot; you travel on the wings of the wind" (Ps 104:2-3) (NAB).

"May the glory of the Lord endure forever; may the Lord rejoice in his works! He who looks upon the earth, and it trembles; Who touches the mountains, and they smoke! I will sing to the Lord as long as I live; I will sing praise to my God while I have being" (Ps 104:31-33) (NRS).

"The Word became flesh and made his dwelling among us.

We have seen his glory, the glory as of the One and only, who came from the Father, full of grace and truth" (Jn 1:14).

In this place that would indeed become the "outer" Pantry of His Divine Stillness, I set up a special corner to be called my Holy of Holies. Here I enthroned God's Holy Word. Here I fell on my face in awe of the Presence of God about to be revealed in this place.

Blanket my life, O God, in Your precious mercy and in Your steadfast love. Great is Your faithfulness. Your mercy is new every morning.

Holy God, without You no one is holy! Only in You and through You can we forsake our sinful ways and become holy like unto You. Your command is: "Be holy as I am holy." All Holy God, we beg You today for the grace to be holy as You are holy.

2

SHOW ME YOUR GLORY

**The Lord said to Moses, "This request, too, which you
have just made, I will carry out, because you have
found favor with me and you are my intimate friend."**
(Ex 33:17-18) (NAB)

AS FOR MOSES IN HIS SINAI DESERT, so for me in my "Pantry of
Divine Stillness," more than anything else the cry of my heart
was: "Lord, show me Your Glory!"

I began to experience the glory of God's presence in the
ordinary—much more than in the extraordinary. I would stop
short in the middle of very ordinary things like rearranging the
cottage, plucking dried leaves from the foliage, reading my mail,
to realize it was more than "mine"—it was "ours!"

Together then, Jesus and I, would rearrange, trim, read and
celebrate the good news. Together in the early morning we
would walk along the shoreline giving praise to the Creator of
such beauty. Together we would shop for the necessary groceries
to keep my body and soul together. Together we related to the
Father and together we cried out for an ever greater increase in
the gifts and power of the Holy Spirit, the manifestation of the
glory of the Father.

The awesome presence of God filled every room, every
corner of this place. God spoke easily and often—sometimes a
new word: "You can no longer separate your life from Mine."
Sometimes a word that had already been given: "We are two in
one—Bridegroom and bride in the heart of our Father."

Sometimes a word from the Word:

"The Lord is waiting to show you favor,
    He rises to pity you . . .
He will be gracious to you when you cry out,
    as soon as he hears he will answer you.
No longer will your Teacher hide himself,
    but with your own eyes you shall see your
    Teacher.

While from behind, a voice shall sound in your ears:
'This is the way; walk in it.'
when you would turn to the right or to the left"
(Is 30:18-21) (NAB).

Like Isaiah, realizing God's holiness and my sinfulness, I would pray for the purifying coal of the seraphim to cleanse my lips and further prepare me for the acceptance of this call on my life. "Here I am Lord! Send me!"

In moments like these, Steve Fry's song filled my space:
"Oh, the glory of Your presence,
we Your temple give You reverence.
So arise from Your rest and be blest by our praise,
as we glory in Your embrace,
as Your presence now fills this place."
(Steve Fry ©1983 Birdwing Music/Cherry Lane Pub.)

Lord, show me Your glory in the very center of my being. By Your Holy Spirit, show me that You reign on the throne of my heart. Show me what separates my life from Your presence within me. Alert me whenever I have spent some time unaware of Your indwelling presence, Father, Son, and Holy Spirit. Stir me to own my independence and separation from You in a prayer of repentance.

I desire to walk, to talk with You as Your great saints and Moses walked and talked with You. Show me when and how I fall short of Your glory that I may quickly come before You to ask Your mercy and Your forgiveness. Amen.

3

SHEKINAH GLORY

Then the cloud covered the meeting tent, and the glory of the Lord filled the Dwelling.

(Ex 40:34) (NAB)

TRULY THE GLORY OF GOD was on that place in Oahu just as the Glory of God was on that place in the land of Egypt.

Like Moses, I could hear the call: "Fran! Fran!"

Like Moses, I answered back: "Here I am."

"Remove the sandals from your feet for the place where you stand is holy ground. I am the God of your father, the God of Abraham, the God of Isaac, the God of Jacob."

Like Moses, I removed the sandals from my feet. This is holy ground. I knew it. I sang it. I hid my face for I, too, was afraid to look at God.

Yet I knew that the Shekinah glory of God—God's visible manifestation of majesty in power, which once filled the tabernacle (Ex 40:34)—was on this place. As truly as Moses knew that he was called to receive commandments from God for the Chosen People of 1300 B.C., I knew that I was being called to receive words from God so that you, the Chosen People of God of this twentieth century and the new millennium, might know that our God is the same yesterday, today, and forever. He is a Holy God. He calls us to be holy as He is holy. "Be holy as I am holy" (1 Pt 1:16). He has neither forsaken nor forgotten you.

Your God has a plan for your well-being. He is a God of glory with power not only to reveal His glory but to transform you into His likeness with ever-increasing glory. He will be there for you. Be there for Him.

"All of us, gazing on the Lord's glory with unveiled faces, are being transformed from glory to glory into his very image by the Lord who is the Spirit" (2 Cor 3:18) (NAB).

"O God, here I am." I cry out to You from my desert spot like Moses cried: "Here I am!" My heart cries out to You in faith, hope and love. I believe in Your love for me and for all peoples. I trust in the power of that love to transform me into Your likeness with ever increasing glory.

You who have begun a good work in me will bring it to completion, in Your own time, in Your own way, and for Your own glory. There is nothing I can do that will bring about this total transformation of myself into Yourself. There is nothing You cannot do, when I allow myself to rest in Your heart and in Your hands, trusting in Your power and Your mercy.

4

REVELATIONS OF GLORY

**Now if we are children, then we are heirs—heirs of
God and co-heirs with Christ, if indeed we share his
sufferings in order that we may also share in his glory.
I consider that our present sufferings are not worth
comparing with the glory that will be revealed to us.**

(Rom 8:17-18)

I AWAKENED TO THE QUIET SWISH of ocean waters. I am here! My
mind is registering the fact that "here" is a strange new place,
thousands of miles from the security of my convent home and
thousands of miles from the comfort of my Sisters, friends and
family.

I am to be alone with my God for thirty days and thirty
nights! Alone!

Suddenly I am remembering another time when I was alone
with God—Father, Son, and Holy Spirit—for ninety days and
ninety nights writing *We, the Bride.*

It was one of the hardest things that I had ever done!

Yet at the same time, it was one of the most beautiful, most
powerful, and unforgettable! There were days when I felt like
Moses eating the sands of the Sinai desert; others when I felt like
Peter, James and John drinking in the glory of Tabor; others when
I felt like John, the Apostle, reminiscing on the Isle of Patmos.

As I stood absorbing the iridescent beauty and the rising
sound of ocean waters, Jesus spoke this word: "Of all the relationships we have with Him, the only one that will last for all
eternity is that He is the Bridegroom and we are the Bride."

"Then I saw a new heaven and a new earth. The former
heaven and the former earth had passed away, and the sea was
no more. I also saw the holy city, a new Jerusalem, coming down
out of heaven from God, prepared as a bride adorned for her hus-
band. I heard a loud voice from the throne saying, 'Behold, God's
dwelling is with the human race. He will dwell with them and

they will be his people and God himself will always be with them'" (Rv 21:1-3) (NAB).

Like Paul I prayed: "May the God of our Lord Jesus Christ, the Father of glory, give you a spirit of wisdom and revelation resulting in the knowledge of him. May the eyes of your hearts be enlightened, that you may know what is the hope that belongs to his call, what are the riches of glory in his inheritance . . . and what is the surpassing greatness of his power for us who believe" (Eph 1:17-20) (NAB).

This is a word of hope for the very difficult times in which we are living. To know who we are as Bride and who Jesus is as the Bridegroom is to stand at the threshold of a new unlimited understanding and release of His glory!

Almighty and Eternal God, only You by the power of Your Holy Spirit can give to us a revelation of Who You are and who we are. In these very special times in which we are living, only You can teach us what it is that You are doing and what it is that You want us to do. You are the Bridegroom and we are the Bride! By Your Holy Spirit reveal to us what that means and empower us to live out that love relationship with You now and for all eternity.

Thank You for the promise that if we share in Your sufferings we will also share in Your glory. In our greatest sufferings, help us to remember that what we suffer at this present time cannot compare with the glory to be revealed to us.

5

PROPHETS OF GLORY

And the glory of the Lord will be revealed, and all mankind together will see it for the mouth of the Lord has spoken.

(Is 40:5)

I FELT LIKE MOSES being called to the top of Mt. Sinai. "And the glory of the Lord settled on Mount Sinai. For six days the cloud covered the mountain, and on the seventh day the Lord called to Moses from within the cloud" (Ex 24:16).

Before I left Milwaukee, the Lord led me to bring along as a plan and a discipline a concordance listing of all the Scriptures containing the word, *glory.* Some four hundred full-blown Scriptures were ready to be absorbed into my spiritual being for whatever they might teach, exhort, or reveal.

"Indeed, the word of God is living and effective, sharper than any two-edged sword, penetrating even between soul and spirit, joints and marrow, and able to discern reflections and thoughts of the heart. No creature is concealed from him, but everything is naked and exposed to the eyes of him to whom we must render an account" (Heb 4:12-13) (NAB).

Beginning with Genesis, I boldly prayed that God would reveal to me that same glory that Adam and Eve knew in Paradise, that Abraham, Isaac, Jacob, and Joseph knew in the land of Canaan.

I praised God for a prayer language that could project me back in time to the Book of Genesis where I could praise Yahweh for the glory that was on all the descendants of Abraham and Sarah, Isaac and Rebekah, Jacob and Rachel, and especially Joseph. Joseph's life and gifted ministry in the land of Egypt was filled with glory and honor.

Not only was I able to pray through the mystery of Yahweh's incredible love and miraculous care for Joseph, but through my prayer language I was enabled to enter into that love and to experience a deeper and richer relationship with Yahweh Himself.

Yahweh's love and faithfulness is celebrated in Jacob's song in Genesis: "Joseph is a fruitful tree by a spring whose branches climb over the wall. The archers savagely attacked him. . . . But Joseph's bow remained unfailing and his arms were tireless by the power of the Strong One of Jacob, by the name of the Shepherd of Israel, by God Almighty, so may he bless you, with the blessings of the heavens above, and the blessings of the deep that lies below. The blessings of breast and womb, and the blessings of your father are stronger than the blessings of the eternal mountains, and the bounty of the everlasting hills. May they rest on the head of Joseph . . ." (Gn 49:22-26) (REB).

Together with the Scriptures of old, songs of old took on new meaning, power and glory.

"Jacob bought a coat, a multi-colored coat to wear.
Joseph's coat was elegant, the cut was fine.
The tasteful style was the ultimate in good design.
And this is why it caught the eye.
A king stopped and stared and when Joseph tried it on he knew his sheepskin days were gone.
Such a dazzling coat of many colors."

"Joseph and the Amazing Technicolor Dreamcoat" was a song for me to sing, a melody for me to bask in. Tim Rice and Andrew Lloyd Weber's musical speaks to us today of the glory of God revealed in Joseph's life and the glory about to be revealed in us. Indeed the blessings of the God of glory are waiting to be poured out upon us, as we realize that our "sheepskin days" are gone.

God of Abraham, Isaac, Jacob, Joseph, God of glory, reveal Yourself anew to me today as You did to Jacob and his favorite son, Joseph. Reveal Yourself to me as You did to Isaiah when You promised "the glory of the Lord will be revealed and all humankind together will see it."

I say "Yes" to that revelation whenever You are ready. I pray for it with the words from Genesis that You pour out on my life this day "blessings of the heavens above, and the blessings of the deep that lies below, the blessings of the everlasting mountains, and the bounty of the eternal hills"
(Gn 49:25-26) (REB).

6

LIGHT, MERCY, GLORY

Arise, shine, Jerusalem, for your light has come, and over you the glory of the Lord has dawned. Though darkness covers the earth and dark night the nations, on you the Lord shines and over you his glory will appear.

(Is 60:1,2) (REB)

LIKE MOSES I cried out to God: "Who am I? Who am I that I should receive this book on Your glory? Who am I that I should expect You to speak to me words for Your people? Who am I that the Shekinah Glory should come down on me again and again. Who am I that . . ." Often before I would give God a chance to answer, I would pray through in my prayer language what I could not understand or comprehend in English.

It was part of a process to take me from where I was, to where God would lead me so I could in His time receive all that He desired to give.

After praying for extended times in my prayer language or "tongues," God was able to speak to me as in His own words from Exodus: "God said to Moses, 'I AM WHO I AM. . . .Thus you shall say to the Israelites, I AM has sent me to you'" (Ex 3:14) (NRS).

"Just as I could deliver My Chosen People out of the grip of a Pharaoh so I can deliver you, My Chosen People of this twentieth century, of the third millennium, from the grip of Satan and all that could cause you to destroy yourselves. I am your Deliverer and I can deliver you but you must be connected to Me. You must turn away from your sin and the works of darkness in your life if you are to be filled with My light and My glory.

"My child, you must discern the battle. You cannot walk with one foot in each kingdom. You cannot walk with one part of you in darkness and the other part in light. If you are to be a child of light you must walk wholly in light. Repent of everything that is a work of darkness. Darkness cannot exist in My light.

"As you cast it out, you enter into the center of the battle around you, the battle against the Kingdom of darkness. I give you My eyes to see and My ears to hear. I give you My mind to discern, that you may walk totally in Me as a child of light. This is a new season. There is no turning back. There is only going forward with your eyes upon Jesus, your mind and heart set like flint to go like Jesus to the cross."

Holy God, Father, Son and Holy Spirit, I ask Your mercy and Your forgiveness for myself, my family, my church, my nation, the nations of the world for all the ways we have fallen short of the glory by allowing the powers of sin and darkness to take over in our lives.

O God, in miracle measure, show us Your sweet mercy! As a people and as a nation we have sinned against You. We have fallen short of the glory. Forgive all our wrongdoing! Jesus, in Your Name, with Your Blood, with Your Word, with the authority You give us as believers, we break the generational bondages of sin and sickness on our lives! You are our holiness and our healer. Father, Son, and Holy Spirit, reveal again to us Your great glory!

Your promise to us in Isaiah is: "Though darkness covers the earth and dark night the nations," You will shine in our lives and Your glory will appear over us.

Thank You for forgiving our sin, breaking our bondages, and pouring forth Your glory upon us. Thank you for the glory that is and will be revealed in us.

7

MORE LIGHT

Rise up in splendor! Your light has come, the glory of the Lord shines upon you. See, darkness covers the earth and thick clouds the peoples; but upon you the Lord shines and over you appears his glory.

(Is 60:1-3) (NAB)

THIS WAS THE FIRST SCRIPTURE I opened my Bible to in 1969 after I had been prayed with for the fullness of the Holy Spirit. "Your light has come. The glory of the Lord shines upon you."

Was it simple for me? No! Any resistance you might have, I had in capital letters with rows of exclamation marks!!!! I was really backward about going forward. Really down on what I wasn't up on! Visions! Prophecy! Tongues! The Word!

Jesus said, "I am the light of the world. Whoever follows me will not walk in darkness" (Jn 8:12). But I was walking in darkness. This little light of mine, I wouldn't let it shine.

The block for me was a stuffy intellect, self-righteousness, pride, fear, a whole litany of defenses. My need was to have someone pray with me for whatever it was God wanted to give me that I didn't have. My need was to acknowledge Jesus anew as the Lord and Savior of my life, to ask Jesus to release in me the fullness of the Holy Spirit from my Baptism and Confirmation, to know the Holy Spirit as the Fullness of three L's—Life, Light, and Love: God's Life, God's Light, God's Love!

I needed to know God's Light and God's Glory on new levels so my life could be a beam of light for others!

A question we might ask ourselves today is: Is there anything blocking my light?

Today's word is: "Arise, shine, for your light has come, and the glory of the Lord rises upon you" (Is 60:1).

Jesus, You said to Your apostles and You are saying to us today: "Many prophets and kings desired to see what you see, but did not see it and to hear what you hear but did not hear it" (Lk 10:24) (NAB).

What are we seeing—renewal, restoration, revival! People like me, families, churches like mine are seeing You, Jesus. You are the light of the world! You are the light of our lives! Your light casts out all darkness!

Jesus, Savior, Healer, Deliverer, light of the world, save us, heal us, deliver us. Light up my life! Defend us against all the assaults of the Powers of Darkness.

Your light has come anew into my life this day. Your glory has dawned anew on my life. Jesus, though darkness covers the earth and thick clouds the people, You shine over me and Your glory appears.

Flood Your light and Your glory this day over all I love and over all for whom I am called to pray. Light of the nations, shine on us. Let Your light in me shine! Shine! Shine!

8

MERCY, HEALING, AND GLORY

And I saw the glory of the God of Israel coming from the east. His voice was like the roar of rushing waters, and the land was radiant with his glory.

(Ez 43:2)

"THE GLORY OF THE LORD shall rest upon you and your city. Have I not given My angels charge over you? And shall I not send forth in this time of darkness a force of My angelic hosts to guard you, to fight for you, to be for you a mighty force against the powers of darkness?

"I am still the Great I AM. I am able to do all that needs to be done. If I can roll back the waters of the Red Sea, then I can roll back the dread sicknesses, the plague of AIDS, the curse of abortion, that is on the nations of the world. Remember nothing is impossible for Me! Nothing is beyond My power! Nothing is beyond My love for you!

"I call you to believe in My love for you, to believe in My goodness and to believe in My mercy. This is the Age of Mercy."

At Notre Dame on June 15, 1974, the night of the historical first healing service for a Catholic Charismatic Convention, I was among the forty thousand standing in the rain, drenched and deeply moved by the healing power of God that moved over that assembly through the prayers of Barb Shlemon and Sister Briege McKenna.

"The Lord wants each one of us to believe He will heal them. As He leaves He wants to look back over Notre Dame as He looked back over the towns He left, knowing He had healed every single person there. If you need healing from sin, if you are troubled in spirit, He desires to heal you. If you have any anguish, any fear, any broken relationships, any sickness that doctors have given up on—He wants to heal you. Any money or job problems—He wants to heal now. The deepest healing many of us need is to know how much Jesus loves us."

Many accounts have been written of that night with varying degrees of skepticism, belief, and unbelief. Attempts have been made to explain what happened. The important thing is not the numbers healed or the kinds of diseases healed, but that as a people of God we were willing to let go of all that was darkness and to move into the marvelous Kingdom of Light.

The important thing was that forty thousand believers were moving in the flow of the Spirit, aware that Jesus was present in that stadium as the Healing Light of the World. They were aware that Jesus was speaking to them through two women using the word of knowledge as they called out numerous diseases that were being healed at that very moment.

"Liver damage, cancer, leukemia, arthritis, problems contracted because of alcohol disease are being taken from the stadium. Stand firm in the faith that God's power is rushing through your nervous system as you are being healed of neurological difficulties. Heart trouble . . . the Lord is being faithful to you because you were faithful to Him when the world said there was no hope.

"Jesus is giving sight to the blind. Feel the healing light penetrate. The haze is being obliterated. Things obscure are being made clear.

"Healings are coming so fast that no power in heaven or on earth can stop what is going on. Epileptics come under the healing power of God.

"A baby in the womb seven months with RH-factor blood type is being changed. There's a family of four with a blood disease—at this moment the blood is being changed."

"There were also many other things that Jesus did; but if these were to be described individually, I do not think the whole world would contain the books that would be written" (Jn 21:25) (NAB).

"The following sung first in tongues and then with interpretation speaks of why God would desire to heal with such marvelous extravagance. 'I have mercy. I have mercy. I have wonderful mercy. I want to wash your feet. I want to heal you. I want to come into your heart. Open yourselves to Me and let Me come in. I want to heal you tonight. I have mercy on you.'"

God of Mercy and God of Glory, God of miracles Who moved in such miraculous power over the people in Notre Dame stadium, I surrender my life to You today for whatever healings I need. You are the Great I AM. I choose this day to walk in Your light as a child of the light. I choose to believe in Your goodness and Your mercy for the healings that I need today and for healings for all those I love and for whom I have been asked to pray.

Defend me against all the assaults of the Powers of Darkness. God of mercy, have mercy on me. Flood my life with Your mercy, healing and glory.

Let the full power of Jesus' life, death, and Resurrection flow into me and through me. Like Jesus, I set my mind and my heart like flint to go to the Cross, and to receive Your forgiveness, mercy, and healing.

9

OLYMPIC GLORY

**And when the Chief Shepherd appears, you will
receive the crown of glory that will never fade away.**

(1 Pt 5:4)

No matter where I land on the face of the earth, New York, Chicago, London, Israel, Hawaii, I know of no better way to be constantly ready for an experience of glory than to begin each day with Spiritual Olympics.

The formula for the Olympics is P = P - I or your Performance equals your Potential minus the Interference. Your potential is to do all that Jesus did and greater things.

I begin as I hold up my Franciscan cross and proclaim anew the Lordship of Jesus Christ. Like Paul: "I prefer to know nothing but Jesus Christ, the Crucified," the power and the glory of God! Before I leave my bedroom the glory comes down! The power comes down! The gifts are set in motion!

Then I bind all the Powers of Darkness that could block the Lordship of Jesus Christ in the lives of all I am called to minister to. I have power from Jesus, King of glory, to bind the demonic powers. "And these signs will accompany those who believe: In My name they will drive out demons, they will speak in new tongues" (Mk 16:17).

Just because we live at a time of which they say, "All the demons have been loosed across the face of the earth," we do not need to live in the heat of daily battles or the torment of fear that we are not going to make it through the struggles. Jesus has already won the victory, the power, and the glory for us on the Cross. We make the choice to be under the doom and the gloom or to be under the power and the glory.

Next I ask for a new Baptism in the Holy Spirit in a different way each day. "Jesus, You are the only one who can do this for me. Baptize me anew in Your Holy Spirit. I want more than a few drops or thoughts of wisdom, truth, love, glory . . . I want an immersion in them like in the Upper Room, and at the River Jordan."

A Baptism is an immersion. It can make all the difference in the world for the power in which we operate. It has been said in business that most people use only ten per cent of their potential. If this is true, how much more true can it be in spiritual sense? We operate on ten per cent of what we could be doing with the gifts, the power, the fruit of the Spirit within us. We operate on a mere ten per cent of the power, the gifts, the glory that could be ours if we truly allowed the release of the Holy Spirit within us.

Again, the formula for the Olympics is $P = P - I$. Your Performance equals your Potential minus the Interference. If our Performance has been lacking, perhaps it is because we are not really in touch with our Potential and we haven't taken care of the Interference.

As a Christian, your Potential is in Matthew, Mark, Luke, John, Philippians, Colossians, Corinthians, Ephesians, Romans, Revelation, the whole of God's Word. Your Potential is to lay your hands on the sick, and they will recover. Your Potential is to bind and to cast out evil, not to live with demonic power or evil plaguing you! Your Potential is in the fullness of God's word.

Jesus, You are my Shepherd. Help me this day and every day of my life to be in touch with my potential, to allow You to live Your life in me, to do my Spiritual Olympics before I leave my bedroom.

Keep me wise to the Interference from the world, the flesh and the devil.

Like Paul, I choose to let go of the rubbish in my life and to stand with You in my choice of "the crown of glory that will never fade away."

10

BLOCKING THE GLORY

There is cause for rejoicing here. You may for a time have to suffer the distress of many trials: but this is so that your faith, which is more precious than the passing splendor of fire-tried gold, may by its genuineness lead to praise, glory, and honor when Jesus Christ appears. Although you have never seen him, you love him, and without seeing you now believe in him, and rejoice with inexpressible joy touched with glory because you are achieving faith's goal, your salvation.

(1 Pt 1:6:9) (NAB)

ONE MORE TIME your performance equals your potential minus the interference.

Peter speaks of our faith coming under the firing line causing us the distress of many trials as we deal with interference from the world, the flesh, and the devil. Each of us has our problems with the world, the flesh and the devil. God's Word speaks about our dealing with them.

"The world with its seductions is passing away but the person who does God's will endures forever" (1 Jn 2:17) (NAB).

"Everyone begotten of God conquers the world" (1 Jn 5:4) (NAB). Have you ever thought of yourself as a "world conqueror?" Paul declares: "Yet in all this we are more than conquerors because of him who has loved us" (Rom 8:37) (NAB).

As for our flesh, Paul says: "Crucify it." "If you live according to the flesh you will die" (Rom 8:13).

"So I say, live by the Spirit and you will not gratify the desires of the sinful nature" (Gal 5:16). "For all men are like grass, and all their glory is like the flowers of the field; the grass withers and the flowers fall, but the Word of the Lord stands forever" (1 Pt 1:24).

Finally, if we are to have the victory over our flesh we need to ask: How often is my flesh nourished with the Bread of Life, the Body and Blood of the Word made Flesh? To receive Communion often is to block the interference and to release the glory.

As for the devil, we have power to bind his power! When we do, what a difference because we have stood in the place of authority and have bound every authority and every power that would come against us.

We battle not with flesh and blood but against Principalities and Powers. In 1 Peter 5:8, we read: "Your enemy the devil prowls around like a roaring lion looking for someone to devour." He goes around like a lion, but he is not one. Jesus is the Lion of the tribe of Judah. In Him we have victory! We have power! And God has the glory!

"One of our greatest needs is to believe in a personal devil even as we believe in a personal God" (Pope Paul VI). There are more than one hundred twenty references about the devil in Scripture, most of them in the New Testament. Jesus was tempted by the devil for forty days. When Jesus cast out the devil, the mute spoke, those possessed were set free, unclean spirits came forth, all who were oppressed by demons were freed.

If we do not bind his powers and take the authority we have as believers, we will have to fight the powers. I do not have time to fight battles that have already been fought for me! The battle belongs to the Lord!

If Jesus came today to give out medals, Gold, Silver, Bronze, for your performance as a Christian, what kind would you get? Athletes from all over the world sweat, strain and stretch as they 'Go for the Gold.' When it comes to God's medals, which one would you get?

Father, Son, and Holy Spirit, I really desire to live up to the fullness of my potential. I ask Your help against the interference. Thank You for providing for my battle with the world, my flesh, and the devil. The power is Yours! The battle is Yours! The victory is Yours!

Your Word says that "Your glory shall come like a pent-up river which Your breath drives along." Let Your glory touch my life today. Let that pent-up river of glory sweep over me now.

I ask today for the fullness of life in Jesus Christ! I desire to run the race so as to win not just a perishable crown but an immortal crown of eternal life and glory with You.

I truly desire to "Go for the Gold, God's Gold!" Empower me to be faithful to my Spiritual Olympics every day of my life. I desire not the gold that fades away, but the endless, eternal treasures of glory that never fade!

11

BEHOLD MY GLORY

**. . . And the glory settled on Mount Sinai. For six days
the cloud covered the mountain, and on the seventh
day the Lord called to Moses from within the cloud.**

(Ex 24:16)

ONE OF MY FAVORITE spiritual exercises was to go down to the
oceanfront when the tide was out or just coming in. Claiming the
ocean floor as my priedieu or kneeling bench, I would begin a
time of praise and worship in my prayer language. Often the
praise might have its base in a psalm like Psalm 97, which I loved
to proclaim, first in English, then in many tongues, for all the
nations of the world to be blessed.

"Yahweh is king! Let the earth rejoice; let the many
    isles be glad!
Cloud, black cloud enfolds him,
saving justice and judgement the foundations of his
    throne.
Fire goes before him, sets ablaze his enemies all
    around;
his lightning-flashes light up the world, the earth
    sees it and quakes.
The mountains melt like wax, before the Lord of all
    the earth.
The heavens proclaim his saving justice,
all nations behold Your glory" (Ps 97:1-6) (NJB).

Here I would envision a United Nations Assembly with
nation after nation being called forth to behold the glory of their
Creator God. The USA, Canada, Mexico, the Caribbean, England,
Ireland, Germany, France, Russia, Poland, Italy, Ghana,
Guatemala, Yugoslavia, etc.

Having proclaimed Yahweh's reign over all the earth, I
would then invite the rising tide to sweep over me. As it did, I
claimed the fullness of His mercy on all the nations of the world.

I prayed that they might know the mercy and forgiveness of a just Judge.

Jesus, we, too, claim Your saving power and Your mercy to touch all the nations of the earth, all people that we love. Let Your omnipotent power go forth from our prayer spot today that all may be brought to repentance, conversion and healing. May all nations and all peoples come to know that the Kingdom, the Power and the Glory are Yours forever and ever!

May the mountains of contention, bitterness, fears, prejudices, and angers melt before You. May the glory that settled on Mt. Sinai settle upon our world forever and ever!

12

GLORY OF INTIMACY

All of us, gazing with unveiled faces on the glory of the Lord, are being transformed into the same image from glory to glory as from the Lord who is the Spirit.

(2 Cor 3:18) (NAB)

IN EXODUS 33, we read about God's threat to chastise the Chosen People after they fell into the sin of worshipping the Golden Calf while Moses was up on the mountain receiving the Ten Commandments. It was Moses' intimacy with God that saved the people from a death that was imminent.

"The Lord used to speak to Moses face to face, as one man speaks to another. . . . Moses said to the Lord, 'You, indeed, are telling me to lead this people on; but you have not let me know whom you will send with me. Yet you have said, 'You are my intimate friend,' and also, 'You have found favor with me.' Now, if I have found favor with you, do let me know your ways so that, in knowing you, I may continue to find favor with you.

" 'I, Myself,' the Lord answered, 'will go along, to give you rest' " (Ex 33:11-14) (NAB).

Father George Maloney, S.J., says in his book, *Intimacy with God*, "Sometimes as we get older people say, 'You are on the way out.' "No," he says, "You are on the way in. The older you get the greater capacity you have for intimacy with God."

God has given me this slogan, "Whatever leads to intimacy go for it. Whatever doesn't, who needs it!"

Dear God, it was Moses' intimacy with You that saved Your people from a death that was imminent. We come to You today with precious memories of all the times You showed Yourself our intimate friend in personal prayer, in times of communion, in studying Your Word, in just being in Your

Presence. For the sake of Your intimacy with us, have mercy on Your people, Your churches, our nation and the nations of the world.

We, too, would like to continue to find favor with You as Moses did. We, too, would like to continue to be Your intimate friends. We, too, choose to "stand in the gap" as Moses did. We stand in a spirit of repentance for our nation and the nations of the world. We have sinned and fallen short of Your glory. We ask Your mercy and Your forgiveness. Bring us to total conversion and a more and more intimate relationship with You. Let us see Your Glory!

13

TABORIC GLORY

He took Peter, John, and James and went up to the
mountain to pray. While he was praying his face
changed in appearance and his clothing became
dazzling white. And behold, two men were
conversing with him, Moses and Elijah, who appeared
in glory and spoke of his exodus that he was going to
accomplish in Jerusalem. Peter and his companions
had been overcome by sleep, but becoming fully
awake, they saw his glory. . . .

(Lk 9:28-32) (NAB)

FROM THE GLORY of the *old* we slip today to the glory of the *new,*
the mystery of the Transfiguration. Even as Peter, James, and
John did, in my spirit I can see the face of Jesus shining as the
sun. His clothes are white as snow.

Like Peter, I cry out, "Lord, it is wonderful to be here in this
place where I, too, can hear Your voice, see Your face, and bask in
the sunshine of Your love and Your glory!"

O Lord, it is good to be where I, too, can hear the voice of
the Father saying: "This is my Son, my beloved. You enjoy his
favor. Listen to him."

What a beautiful coincidence that in the first week of my
time away was the Feast of the Transfiguration. "While he was
still speaking, behold, a bright cloud cast a shadow over them,
then from the cloud came a voice that said, 'This is my beloved
Son, with whom I am well pleased; listen to him'" (Mt 17:5)
(NAB).

"As they were coming down the mountainside Jesus commanded them: 'Do not tell anyone of the vision until the Son of
Man rises from the dead'" (Mt 17:9) (NAB).

The contrast hit me like a shaft of Taboric light! The order to
us today is: "Tell everyone! The Good News is way overdue for a
world of about 4.7 billion who still await the full message of Jesus
Christ given almost two thousand years ago. It is almost two

thousand years since Jesus is risen from the dead! Who is the last person with whom you shared this Good News?

"Tell everyone not only that Jesus is risen but that He is in the glory of the Father.

"Tell everyone that 'soon and very soon' He will come again in glory!

"Tell everyone that *soon and very soon* we, too, shall be transfigured and share in that eternal glory."

One of the Memorial Acclamations that we proclaim every time we celebrate Eucharist is "When we eat this bread and drink this cup, we proclaim your death, Lord Jesus, until You come in glory." If we truly believe this, we could hardly contain ourselves with the joy of anticipation for the great mystery soon to happen! Our hearts should do a somersault every time "we proclaim your death, Lord Jesus, until You come in glory." We should shout it from the rooftops for all the world to hear! Maranatha! Come, Lord Jesus! Come in Glory!

Jesus, You promised that You would be with us "until the end of time." Thank you for the promise that You are with us in these "end times." We do not fully know what that means. But we know that You are with us in the times we are living in and in the times we are moving toward.

If there is something we need to know, You teach us. If there is some way You want to direct us, You speak to us. If there is a path You want us to follow, You show us. Your promise, Lord Jesus, is that You will be with us no matter what!

Like Peter, James, and John, who saw You in the glory of Your Transfiguration, we, too, have witnessed Your glory in our lives in many big and little ways. Continue to reveal Yourself to us in the glory of Tabor. Give us Your joy as we anticipate Your coming in glory.

Help us particularly at the Memorial Acclamation at Mass to anticipate with great joy the mystery of Your return in glory. Give us the desire to proclaim it from the housetops: "When we eat this bread and drink this cup, we proclaim Your death, Lord Jesus, until You come in glory."

14

LORD JESUS, COME IN GLORY

This is the word of the Lord to Zerubbabel: 'Not by might, nor by power, but by my Spirit says the Lord of hosts.'

(Zec 4:6)

MY GOD SPEAKS TO ME TODAY, as He spoke to Zerubbabel, the prophet, as he was called to build the temple. As I am meditating on these words, I realize the call on my life is not to build a temple but to receive a message.

Not by might, not by power, only by the Spirit of God can any of us receive a message of how to ready our hearts, our minds, our spirits for His soon return. There is no holding back the springtime. There is no holding back the soon return of Jeshua!

We cannot stop it but we can hasten it. Every time we allow our hearts to cry out: "Maranatha! Come, Lord Jesus!" Jeshua is closer!

Write it across the doorway of your house. "Maranatha! Come, Lord Jesus! Come! Come in glory!"

Write it across your prayer room and churches. "Come, Lord Jesus! Come!"

Write it across your heart! Emblazon it in light! Let it penetrate the darkness! "Come, Lord Jesus! Come in glory! Come, Lord Jesus! Come!"

As John cried out in the conclusion of the Book of Revelations: "Come, Lord Jesus. Come" (Rev 22:20).

Let us cry out together with the nations of the world from across Europe, Asia, Africa, Australia, North America, South America. "Come, Lord Jesus! Come in glory!" Together with every nation, tribe, and background, let us shout it! "Come, Lord Jesus! Come in glory!"

Only by Your Spirit, Lord, can we know what it means for us to prepare our hearts and our lives for Your coming again in glory. By Your Spirit reveal to us what it is that You are doing so that we can do it with You.

By Your Spirit build each one of us and our churches into a temple pleasing in Your sight. Not by might, not by power, but by Your Spirit we pray that all this be done for Your greater honor and glory!

By Your Spirit enable us to let go of all that is not You, so that we may ever more readily move with what is You! Quicken in our hearts and in our spirits the cry: "Maranatha! Come, Lord Jesus! Come!"

TRANSFORMATION INTO GLORY

> **Think of the love that the Father has lavished on you
> by letting you be called God's children. That is what
> you are, but what we are to be in the future, as the
> Bride of Jesus, has not yet been revealed. All we
> know is that when it is revealed, we shall all be like
> our Bridegroom because we shall see him as he really
> is. Surely everyone who entertains this hope must try
> to be pure as our Bridegroom is pure, to live a holy
> life, to be holy just as he is holy.**
>
> (Jn 3:1-3,7, my paraphrase)

"DEAR FRIENDS, now we are children of God and what we will be has not yet been made known. But we know that when he appears, we shall be like him, for we shall see him as he is" (1 Jn 3:2). What if this happened next year, in five years, ten years, twenty years? Would you be ready and willing for so great a change in your life?

Whether we are ready and willing, agree or not agree, God is going to keep right on doing what He is doing. We can either move with Him in His measure of grace and glory or we can miss God. It is possible to miss the moving of your God.

We shall see Jesus, the Son of the living God as Peter, James, John and all the Apostles saw Him; as Mary, His Mother, and all the holy women saw Him. We shall see Him as He is and we shall be like Him.

"Soon and very soon!" This is our hope. This is the Good News! This was the reason for my being called to Hawaii to receive words to encourage you to ask God for this transformation in your life. I was called that you might more clearly hear and more quickly respond to the call that is on your life—that you might see beyond the darkness that is threatening our lives and live in the glorious hope of His Second Coming in glory.

"For when Christ is revealed we shall all be like him in glory, for we shall see him as he is in glory." This is no new revelation. This is something to which we want to say an ongoing yes, that nothing may halt or hinder the perfect timing of Jesus' coming in glory!

To believe that it is happening now, today, tomorrow, next week is challenging! To believe that we are being transformed into that eternal glory that we will be in for all eternity is daring. "All of us, gazing with unveiled faces on the glory of the Lord, are being transformed into the same image from glory to glory as from the Lord who is the Spirit" (2 Cor 3:18) (NAB). It is the same glory but in the embryonic stage. "Let all that is within us cry 'Glory!'"

The two most common prophecies across the face of the earth are: (1) the imminent return of Jesus Christ; and (2) power will not be lacking to you for the work God calls you to do.

At Mass every day, we proclaim: "When we eat this bread and drink this cup, we proclaim your death, Lord Jesus, until You come in glory."

Just as we saw the fall of the Berlin Wall and the collapse of Communist Russia (neither of which we really anticipated seeing in our lifetime), I believe we are going to see Jesus Christ return as He really is "in glory!" And we shall be like Him!

I pray this day to listen to the voice of Jesus as My Father bids me to do. "'This is my Son, whom I love; with him I am well pleased. Listen to him!'" (Mt 17:5).

Looking up we see no one but You, Jesus! We see You, Jesus, Son of God, Who was, Who is, and Who is to come again in great power and glory. We see You, Jesus, the beginning, the end, and all the in-betweens. We see You, Jesus, as Peter, James, and John saw You on the Holy Mount and our hearts cry out like Peter's: Lord, it is good for us to be here this day in our prayer time. It is good to know that You are fully in charge and that nothing is impossible for You.

Help us to live that pure and holy life so that we might become more and more like You, our Bridegroom. Pure like You! Holy like You!

Jesus for almost two thousand years, You are living to make intercession for us in the Presence of the Father. You are an offering for our sins. "Not only for our sins" as John tells us in his letter, "but for those of the whole world." We join in Your prayer and intercession this day for the sins of the whole world especially the sins we have been aware of on our TVs, in our newspapers and in our news magazines. With Jesus we pray, "Father, forgive them for they know not what they do."

16

GLORIOUSLY TRIUMPHANT

I will sing to the Lord, for he is gloriously triumphant; horse and chariot he has cast into the sea. My strength and courage is the Lord; and he has been my savior. He is my God. I praise him; the God of my Father, I extol him. The Lord is a warrior, Lord is his name! . . .Your right hand, O Lord, is magnificent in power, your right hand, O Lord, has shattered the enemy. . . . Who is like you among the gods, O Lord? Who is like to you, magnificent in holiness?

(Ex 15:1-3, 6, 11) (NAB)

MOSES AND THE ISRAELITES sang this song to the Lord. What a way to connect with our Jewish roots. What a way to sing to the Lord today, as we move toward the year 2000, the song Moses and the Israelites sang over three thousand years ago. "I will sing to the Lord for He is gloriously triumphant!" In my life this day, He is and will be gloriously triumphant! Over every power of darkness, He will be gloriously triumphant!

"Your right hand is magnificent in power. The Lord is a warrior." I am not the warrior. I can expect the Lord to go to battle for me. I can pray and then sit back to watch the incredible operations of victory by my God.

"Who is like You among the gods, who is like You, magnificent in holiness?" This is the God I want to identify my life with, to entrust my life to. A God who is magnificent in holiness! Gloriously triumphant! Beyond a Lorenzo the Magnificent! My God is matchless in power and glory!

The same God who brought Moses and the Israelites victory is the One who will shatter my enemies today! I believe it!

The same God who caused this song to break forth for the Israelites as they triumphantly marched through the Red Sea is the One who will reveal Himself to me today, tomorrow, forever!

Father, Son, and Holy Spirit, You are the same yesterday, today, and forever. This day we sing the same song of triumph that Your chosen people sang almost three thousand years ago. We acclaim You as Warrior Lord! You are at work in our lives leading us to victory. Your right hand is magnificent in power to deliver us and to shatter all our enemies. Who is like You? No one! You are magnificent in power bringing us to magnificent glory, healing, and holiness! We praise You, O God, for all Your works are wonderful!

To You we sing a song of victory for in You we are victorious over every power that would loot or destroy us.

"Let all your works give you thanks, O Lord, and let your faithful ones bless you.

Let them discourse of the glory of your kingdom and speak of your might,

Making known to men your might and the glorious splendor of your kingdom" (Ps 145:10-12) (NAB).

My strength and my courage is in You for You are my Lord and my personal Savior forever!

17

RUMBLE OF MY GRUMBLE

Then Moses said to Aaron, "Tell the whole Israelite community 'Present yourselves before the Lord for he has heard your grumbling.'" When Aaron announced this to the whole Israelite community, they turned toward the desert and lo the glory of the Lord appeared in the cloud!

(Ex 16:9-10) (NAB)

THAT SAME GOD who appeared in the cloud despite the grumbling of the Israelites is the God Who manifests Himself in glory to us today. Despite our grumblings our God will be there for us.

Recently a man on the phone was being very obnoxious to me in his claims for justice that really were not just. As I prayed, God called me to let go of the scales of justice which, in my judgment, were swinging high in his favor and low in mine.

I would have liked to continue grumbling and to tell the world what a scoundrel the man is. God was asking me to let go of the earthly scales of justice and allow His eternal scales of justice to work it out.

It was not easy, but I did it. And I know that God did it—worked it out in ways far beyond my fondest dreaming or scheming.

O Lord God, forgive us for the many times when we might have praised You, but have turned to resentment and grumbling. In Your Word, You advise that we "praise You in all circumstances." Help us to do just that especially when our circumstances are such that we are inclined to grumble.

Oh, God, stop the rumble of my grumble!

Lift the voice of praise. We praise You, O God, for all Your works are wonderful! Wonder full! Full of WONDER!!

18

CONSUMING FIRE GLORY

The Lord said to Moses, 'Come up to me on the mountain and, while you are there, I will give you the stone tablets on which I have written the commandments intended for their instruction.' . . . The glory of the Lord settled upon Mt. Sinai. The cloud covered it for six days, and on the seventh day God called to Moses from the midst of the cloud. The glory of the Lord was seen as a consuming fire on the mountain top. But Moses passed into the midst of the cloud and he went up on the mountain; and there he stayed for forty days and forty nights.

(Ex 24:12, 16-18) (NAB)

I AM IN AWE that the same God who manifested His glory to Moses on Mt. Sinai for forty days and forty nights is the God who is manifesting Himself to me today in my prayer pantry. He is the same God who will be here for me for thirty days and thirty nights. He is the same, majestic in holiness, awesome in glory, a wonder-working God who will enable me to live by the Ten Commandments and all He has directed for my life.

"Then Moses said, 'This is what the Lord has commanded you to do, so that the glory of the Lord may appear to you'" (Lv 9:6).

What is it that the Lord is commanding you to do today so that the glory of the Lord may appear to you, too?

The God of Moses will be with you in your prayer closet today and for as often as you are there. He will enable you to walk in the victory of keeping those Ten Commandments. Can you thank Him for the victory, the power, the glory that will be yours today as you walk in obedience to the Commandments of your God?

"Glory in His holy name, let the hearts of those who seek Him rejoice" (Ps 105:3).

Lord, God, have I ever thanked You for giving the Ten Commandments to us through Moses, Your prophet? Have I ever thanked You for the divine order they have brought into my life? Thank You today for all the ways they have been a blessing to me, to my family, to my Church, to all peoples for all times.

Forgive me for any and every time that I have fallen short of the glory by breaking any of Your commandments. Restore to me the joy and the glory of my salvation now and forever. Forgive my family, my Church, my nation, the nations of the world for all the ways we have sinned against You.

Forgive us as a nation under God for all the ways our laws have ignored Your Laws. Forgive us as a nation for all the ways that we have fallen short of the glory.

Bless us as a nation and enable us to be a blessing to nations less blessed and less fortunate than we are.

"We were therefore buried with him through baptism into death in order that, just as Christ was raised from the dead through the glory of the Father, we too may live a new life" (Rom 6:4).

19

GLORY OF GOD'S PRESENCE

Finally, he set up the court around the Dwelling and the altar and hung the curtain at the entrance of the court. Thus Moses finished all the work. Then the cloud covered the meeting tent, and the glory of the Lord filled the Dwelling. Moses could not enter the meeting tent, because the cloud settled down upon it and the glory of the Lord filled the Dwelling.

(Ex 40:33-35) (NAB)

WE READ DETAIL AFTER DETAIL about the erection of the dwelling of the Lord. It concludes with God's awesome presence in this dwelling, "After Moses had finished all the work as the Lord had told Him to do, God's presence filled the dwelling."

"It is all in My presence." Again I am reminded of the power of His presence today to bring about whatever is in God's will and purpose.

"God is the same yesterday, today and forever." I have discovered again and again that the key to God working in miracle power is to *proclaim God's presence to meet people's needs.* The poorer the people the more powerful God's working.

Recently in Dominica, West Indies, we had a healing service for some 2,500 people. Throughout the service, the healing presence of Jesus was proclaimed again and again.

As we concluded the service I asked all those who had been in some way healed by the presence of Jesus to raise their hand. Instantly a sea of hands arose which could well have been 2,500 hands.

"He went through the villages and He healed everyone."

God is the same yesterday, today, and forever. What Jesus did in the Gospels of Matthew, Mark, Luke, and John, He is doing today in nations, cities, villages, hearts across the face of the earth.

"Whenever the cloud rose from the dwelling, the Israelites would set out on their journey but if the cloud did not lift, they could not go forward. In the daytime the cloud of the Lord was seen over the Dwelling; whereas at night, fire was seen in the cloud by the whole house of Israel in all the stages of their journey" (Ex 40:36-38) (NAB).

"Then the man brought me by way of the north gate to the front of the temple, and when I looked I saw the glory of the Lord filling the Lord's temple, and I fell facedown" (Ez 44:4).

Lord God, how often have we been present when Your awesome presence filled the place of our worship. You are the same yesterday, today and forever. You are the same God who revealed Yourself to Moses, Aaron, and all the people. We bow down before Your presence this day in our lives. We proclaim Your presence to meet our needs.

"And my God will meet all your needs according to His glorious riches in Christ Jesus" (Phil 4:19) (NAB).

There is none like You, O Lord. There is no one who can bring peace, joy, and order in our lives, but You can by Your Spirit. Lord God of Israel and our God, flood us with Your presence and Your glory.

20

VISION OF GLORY

You have enlarged the nation, O Lord; You have
enlarged the nation. You have gained glory for
yourself; You have extended all the borders of the
land.

(Is 26:15)

ON THE DAY of my settling in on the North Shore, Hazel was given this vision and word: "For seven days God would have me on His potter's wheel shaping, fashioning, forming, but most of all enlarging my vessel. In the vision, Hazel saw a vessel that was rather small *enlarge* to at least three times its size. Under it were the words 'before' and 'after.' Above the 'after' vessel there was a chalice pouring forth glory into the vessel."

Indeed for seven days, the Father had me on His Divine Potter's wheel. He did a work of shaping, fashioning, and forming me into a vessel pleasing in His sight so when His time was ready, He would pour forth His glory in whatever way He chose.

"One picture is worth a thousand words." How else can we experience the ongoing glory of God except by ongoing visions for God's people. People without a vision perish. According to tradition, for the first eight hundred years the unusual gifts of the Holy Spirit like visions, tongues, prophecy, and healing were commonly experienced in the Church.

The twentieth century could well be called the Century of the Holy Spirit—with the miraculous outpouring of the gifts of the Holy Spirit at the turn of the century on Azusa Street in California, in 1967 at Duquesne University in Pittsburgh, and most recently in Toronto, Canada, a Holy Spirit Renewal, Restoration and Revival have been set in motion.

In the book of Joel we read: "After this I shall pour forth my Spirit on all humanity. Your sons and daughters shall prophesy, your old people shall dream dreams, and your young people see visions. Even on the slaves, men and women, shall I pour out my spirit in those days. I shall show portents in the sky and on earth. . ." (Jl 3:1-3) (NJB). We are living in the latter days compared to the former days when Joel first spoke about visions and Peter and the early Church experienced them.

God, I thank You for every vision that You have ever given. You are a God who never promises lightly. You have promised the gift of vision for the very difficult times that we are living in and moving toward. That we may understand what is going on in our own hearts and in the world, speak to us in visions and dreams of the night.

Forgive us for all the ways that we have used our minds that could now block the gift of vision. Thank You for forgiving us.

In the Name of Jesus, with the Blood of Jesus, with the Word of Jesus, we free our minds to receive the visions that You would give us for our lives and our Church today.

We blanket our minds with Your Precious Blood, Lord Jesus, that the enemy may not cause contradiction and confusion in what You desire to show us. Enlarge our vessels so that we may hold more and more of Your glory here on earth and forever in heaven.

21

FACE TO FACE GLORY

Who among the gods is like you, O Lord? Who is like you—majestic in holiness, awesome in glory, working wonders?

(Ex 15:11) (NAB)

The glory of the Lord settled on Mount Sinai. For six days the cloud covered the mountain, and on the seventh day the Lord called to Moses from within the cloud. To the Israelites the glory of the Lord looked like a consuming fire on top of the mountain.

(Ex 24:16,17) (NAB)

THE GLORY OF GOD was constantly with Moses in all his dealings with a rebellious people. God appeared to Moses again and again. The Lord showed forth His glory, spoke forth His direction, and filled Moses with His glory.

Despite all the powerful ways God used him, Moses was "the meekest man on the face of the earth." Again and again he had to deal with God's anger toward a disobedient, rebellious people, yet he remained the meek servant of Yahweh and the Chosen People.

Because Moses was such a meek and humble servant, Yahweh could communicate with him as with no other prophet of God. He needed no visions or dreams. Moses experienced God face to face! "Should there be a prophet among you, in visions will I reveal myself to him, in dreams will I speak to him; not so with my servant Moses! Throughout my house he bears my trust: face to face I speak to him, plainly and not in riddles. The presence of the Lord he beholds" (Nm 12:6-8) (NAB).

Father God, Yahweh, be with us as You were with Moses. Speak to us plainly and not in riddles. Unmask our hidden rebellions. Grace us to own our sinfulness that we may be brought to conversion, repentance, and healing. Lord, we pray as Moses prayed, "Show us Your glory." Your Presence we desire to behold.

In visions reveal Yourself to us. In dreams speak to us. Give us the faith to believe that You are here even though we neither see Your face nor hear Your voice. "Help us, O God our Savior, for the glory of Your name; deliver us and forgive our sins for your name's sake" (Ps 79:9).

22

REPENTANCE AND GLORY

For although they knew God they did not accord him glory as God or give him thanks. Instead, they became vain in their reasoning, and their senseless minds were darkened. While claiming to be wise, they became fools and exchanged the glory of the immortal God for the likeness of an image of mortal man or of birds or of four-legged animals or of snakes.

(Rom 1:21-23) (NAB)

Their glory is in their 'shame.' Their minds are occupied with earthly things.

(Phil 3:19) (NAB)

"COME BEFORE ME, My people, in a spirit of repentance. Come!"

We face the ongoing challenge to come before the Living God in a spirit of repentance and allow God to show us what has been sin and rebellion in our lives.

The Chosen People were constantly being called to repentance so Yahweh could reveal His glory to them. We, too, are being called to repentance so Yahweh can reveal His glory to us. Without repentance there can be no glory!

"It is not our sinfulness so much that bothers God; it is what we do to cover it up," our Mother General once shared as we were making a Jubilee retreat in Rome.

To our next "R&R" Rest and Relaxation day, let us add a third "R": Repent! And see in what measure God will pour out His glory on us because we have repented!

God has taught me that "repenting" can be truly High Adventure. While shopping for fresh fruit in the supermarket one day, after carefully making some "good deal" choices, I heard: "Repent for every time that you have gone shopping and rejoiced for the 'good deal' you got, rather than seeing it all as gift from your Father's Hand."

The aisle of the supermarket became my instant church. "That's right, God! That's the way I think! It is me getting a 'good deal' and losing sight of You as my Provider! I am sorry. Thank You for forgiving me!"

Repenting in the supermarket is a different way to live. Judge it by the "fruit that will last": Peace! Joy! Love! GLORY!

Holy God, I come before You today desiring to own and repent of all that has been sin in my life. Whatever! Whenever! Wherever!!

Continue to convict me by Your Holy Spirit! Lead me in ongoing repentance of all the ways I have fallen and continue to fall short of the glory. Bring me as You did Moses, and all Your great saints, Peter, Paul, Mary Magdalene, Augustine, into an ever-growing experience of Your saving grace and glory.

Renew my mind by Your Spirit so that I may quickly shift my thoughts from earthly things to heavenly things.

23

GARBAGE TO GLORY

**This is what the Lord orders you to do that the glory
of the Lord may be revealed to you. Come up to the
altar and offer your sin offering and your holocaust in
atonement for yourself and for your family. Then
present the offering of the people in atonement for
them as the Lord has commanded.**

(Lv 9:6) (NAB)

IN WAYS THAT WERE ENTIRELY DIFFERENT, creative, and "right-brained," I felt the Lord was asking me to bring before Him to the foot of the Cross all that has been sin in my life, sin in my family, sin in my community, sin in my church, sin in the world. "All have sinned and fall short of the glory of God" (Rom 3:23).

As I stood on the shore of the Pacific, I was led to take one Commandment at a time, from the first through the tenth, standing in repentance for every way I or we might have fallen short of the glory by unrepented sin in my life, in my family, in my community, in my Church, and in my nation. Praying in my prayer language, I claimed the power of the Precious Blood, the power of His Holy Name and the power of the Word of God to cleanse us from all wrongdoing. Roll after roll of the mighty ocean waves washing over me were symbolic of the breaking of curses and bondages on our families, cities and nations.

Throughout the prayer, I sensed a great intergenerational cleansing taking place, a loosing and a binding.

"Surely he took up our infirmities and carried our sorrows, yet we considered him stricken by God, smitten by him, and afflicted. But he was pierced for our transgressions, he was crushed for our iniquities; the punishment that brought us peace was upon him, and by his wounds we are healed" (Is 53:4-5).

"For our struggle is not against flesh and blood, but against the rulers, against the authorities, against the powers of this dark world and against the spiritual forces of evil in the heavenly realms" (Eph 6:12).

"For you know that it was not with perishable things such as silver or gold that you were redeemed from the empty way of life handed down to you from your forefathers, but with the precious blood of Christ, a lamb without blemish or defect" (1 Pt 1:18-19).

"Cry out 'Save us, O God our Savior; gather us and deliver us from the nations, that we may give thanks to Your holy name, that we may glory in your praise' " (1 Chr 16:35).

" 'The glory of this present house will be greater than the glory of the former house,' says the Lord Almighty. 'And in this place I will grant peace,' declares the Lord Almighty" (Hg 2:9).

Lord God, even as You called Your Chosen People to repentance so that You might reveal Your glory to them, You call us to repent for every time that we fall short of Your glory. Teach us by Your Spirit what it means to forgive and to be forgiven.

Thank You that the earth is being filled with the knowledge of Your glory as the waters cover the sea. Thank You that the glory that is coming to us and Your Church today will be greater than anything we have ever seen. "And in this place," You have promised through Haggai, Your prophet, "I will grant peace!"

Peace comes from right order. Right order is that You are Lord of our lives. Order our lives under Your Lordship, Lord Jesus. Reveal to us our hidden rebellions. Reveal to us what is garbage in our lives so that You may transform our garbage to glory.

24

FIRE AND GLORY

The glory of the Lord settled on Mount Sinai. For six days the cloud covered the mountain, and on the seventh day the Lord called to Moses from within the cloud. To the Israelites the glory of the Lord looked like a consuming fire on top of the mountain.

(Ex 24:16,17)

"TO THE ISRAELITES the glory of the Lord looked like a consuming fire on top of the mountain" (Ex 24:17).

"What I have not been able to achieve through gifts and power I will achieve through fire and judgment." God spoke this word to the leaders in the Catholic Charismatic Renewal more than a decade ago.

My heart's response was: "God, I do not like fire. I was burnt once. And I do not like judgment. So I will be under the table (not literally) until the fire is over."

Guess what! God found me "under my table," and spoke this word: "Do not fear My fire. It is only the sweet fire of My Holy Spirit. When you say yes to the fire of My Holy Spirit, all you do is allow Me to burn up the rubbish in your life.

"Do not fear My judgment. When you say yes to My judgment in the now, it is a sweet, merciful judgment for I know the rock from which you are hewn. I know the clay from which you are made. I do not expect perfection in the now.

"But I do expect you to say yes to the sweet fire of My Spirit and the merciful fire of My judgment in the now, so that I might reveal to you My glory."

Come Spirit of God! Come with Your sweet, holy fire. Enkindle it in my life. Burn up my rubbish. Purify my heart, my mind, my spirit! Cleanse me from within and make me

holy. Holy as You are holy! Let me be as gold and precious silver.

Come with Your sweet, merciful judgment on my life. This is the Age of Mercy. Mercy means I don't deserve a thing. Of all the gifts, graces, power You have poured into my life, I do not deserve a thing. You just give it because You are a God of mercy. Judge me in the now so that I may never need to fear Your judgment to come. May Your sweet merciful judgment be upon my life, my family, my community, my church, my nation, the nations of the world.

"All of us, gazing with unveiled faces on the glory of the Lord, are being transformed into the same image from glory to glory as from the Lord who is the Spirit" (2 Cor 3:18) (NAB).

25

TONGUES OF GLORY

When my glory passes by, I will put you in a cleft of the rock and cover you with my hand until I have passed by.

(Ex 33:22)

AS FOR MOSES, this promise was there for me. Literally I discovered for myself clefts in the rock, that was the North Shore line, where I could hide and pray as God's glory passed over me.

During my entire stay in Hawaii, no other gift of the Spirit was as practical and useful for me as the gift of tongues. In any one of 2,400 languages of the world I prayed for the needs of the world. Not just a few words, but with the impact of a Ph.D. in my prayer language, I prayed for long, long periods of time. With a confidence that can only come from God, I would lift up the world with all of its need to know the mercy and the glory of God.

Often my prayer was simply worship and praise. Sometimes it was a "new song" in melody and in words. Other times it was pure intercession. One day after receiving the Scripture: "Ask of me and I will give to you the nations for your inheritance" (Ps 2:8) (NAB), I proceeded to pray for a long time asking for nation after nation to know the mercy and the glory of God.

As I would name the nation, I would receive the prayer language of the nation being prayed for. When interceding for Africa, I could almost hear the bongo drums in the background of the Kiswahili sounds.

Like John on Patmos, my "North Shore Prayer Pantry" was a place to exercise all the gifts of the Holy Spirit especially and with ever increasing awareness—my prayer language. It was part of my Great Commission to Hawaii: "You will speak in new tongues." For me that meant: "You will if you will." I willed.

Beyond any other gift, tongues has put me in a whirlwind-love relationship with the Father, Son and Holy Spirit. God's thoughts are above my thoughts like the heavens are above the earth. How else except through this gift could I get on God's "wavelength."

Some time ago in Nebraska, during a teaching and demonstration of the prayer language, I let go a flow of sounds and syllables (tongues). From the back of the room, a "nun" stood up and stated: "I just returned from a mission in Africa. You were just speaking Kiswahili and I understood all of it."

"I was?" I faltered.

"Yes, and this is what you said in Kiswahili: 'My Father is the greatest. He is so powerful, so wonderful, He can do anything! And He will do anything for me because He loves me!'"

I know of no better example of how real this gift is and how it puts us in touch with both Who God is and who we are, what God has done for us, and what God is ready to do for us.

Yes, Father, You are the greatest! You are so powerful, so wonderful. You can do anything and You will do anything for me because You love me. I choose to believe in Your miraculous love for me this day. Manifest it as You will.

Holy Spirit, Spirit of Love, speak for me this day for all the things I don't know how to pray for as I ought.

Jesus, in Your Word, we pray with Paul, every knee shall bow and every tongue confess that Jesus Christ is Lord to the Glory of God, the Father. Amen. (Phil 2:11).

Jesus, this day I bend my knee and confess with my tongue that You are my Lord to the glory of God the Father.

26

MORE TONGUES OF GLORY

**I keep asking that the God of our Lord Jesus Christ,
the glorious Father, may give you the Spirit of
wisdom and revelation, so that you might know him
better.**

(Eph 1:17) (REB)

PRAYING IN A PRAYER LANGUAGE is not unlike infused contempla-
tion. In both the mind is unfruitful. When I pray in tongues, my
prayer does not depend on the use of my mind. It is the "language of the subconscious and unconscious." Psychologists say
that eighty percent of what we are is buried there. How wonderful then in moments of prayer to release all that is buried in our
subconscious and unconscious to God's mind and God's omnipotent healing touch. Having a Master's Degree in psychology, I
sense on a more than ordinary level the depths of the hurts and
bondages that any one of us might have buried there.

Singing and praying in my prayer language for thirty days
and thirty nights had benefits that reach to infinity. There is no
measuring or computing anyone's journey into the heart of God.

The way you pray for it is the way you get it! I have seen
the truth of this in my own life as well as in others. I recall one
priest sharing with me: "I feel I have made more progress in my
prayer life during one month praying in tongues than in the first
twenty years of my priestly life without tongues."

Finally, let me summarize: This is not a "glory gift" that anyone has to have. But it is certainly one that anyone can have if
they want it.

We are living in an age when the big question is: "What sign
were you born under?" I always answer, "The Sign of the Cross."
Jesus never said that we should follow signs. He said that the
signs should follow us.

"These signs will accompany those who believe . . . they will
have the gift of new tongues" (Mk 16:17) (NJB).

Today, Jesus, let it happen in my song, in my spirit, in my heart! Let the signs follow me.

God, this glorious gift of tongues was part of the tradition of the Church for the first 800 years starting in the Upper Room in Jerusalem. Thank You for gifting the early Church and our Church today with such a gift and such power!

In this time of Renewal, Restoration and Revival, restore to all churches all the gifts, all the power, and all the fruit of Your Holy Spirit, especially the gift of tongues! Let Your glory reign on earth as it is in heaven. May all peoples be filled with Your glory. As in the early church, so today may all people glorify and praise You in many tongues. Now and forever!

"These signs will accompany those who believe . . . they will use my name to expel demons, they will speak new languages" (Mk 16:17) (NAB).

"Tongues as of fire appeared, which parted and came to rest on each of them. All were filled with the Holy Spirit. They began to express themselves in foreign tongues and make bold proclamation as the Spirit prompted them" (Acts 2:3-4) (NAB).

27

MORNING DEW GLORY

The whole world before you is like a speck that tips the scales, and like a drop of morning dew that falls on the ground.

(Wis 11:22) (NRS)

GOD'S FAVORITE ONE-LINER to me is "BIG DEAL! How big am I?" God is so big there is nothing beyond His power, nothing beyond His love!

When I have problems I can often trace them back to my taking back the Lordship of Jesus in my life. Even after officially pronouncing Jesus the Lord of my life as early as 7:00 a.m., sometimes by 10:00 a.m. I have "lost my cool." Something I do not like is happening or something I really want to happen is not happening.

As I realize that I have "lost my cool," I hear Jesus saying, "Hey, kid, who is Lord?"

"Ohhh! You are the Lord! Then it is Your problem!" I respond.

I give it to Him—from my hands to His nail-scarred hands.

"Cast your burden upon the Lord and He will sustain you" (Ps 55:23) (NRS).

Cast your burden upon the Lord is a very real command from the mouth of God. One day Jesus challenged me with: "If you want any of your burdens back you have to come and ask Me."

Once-upon-a-God-time I had an unreal burden for an ungodly friend. I kept asking God for the miracle that would change his life until one day God stopped me with: "Make up your mind who has him—you or I. If you have him, I haven't got him. If I have him, you haven't got him. Stop asking and start praising Me for what I am doing in his life."

"You've got him. And I am starting to praise You right now for what You are doing." In a month's time there was a dramatic conversion! Glory!

"Every knee should bend . . . and every tongue confess that Jesus Christ is Lord to the glory of God the Father" (Phil 2:11) (NAB).

There is nothing comparable to starting with your own knee bowing and your own tongue confessing Jesus Christ is Lord in every circumstance for all for whom we pray. If He is Lord, you don't have to be!

It's as simple as that. Big deal!

Jesus, help me to be little so that You can be big. Remind me whenever I am inclined to renege on what I have surrendered to You whether it be time, talents, or money. If You are Lord, I don't have to be. Keep me in my place when I step or speak out of line with Your and my favorite one-liner "Big Deal."

Help me to yield so that You can be the Lord of my life in all its details one hour, one day at a time. Alert me whenever I am taking back Your Lordship over my life. Inspire me by Your Spirit to give it right back to You. Through Your Spirit strengthen me with power in my inner being so that I might truly live my life in all its details under Your glorious and eternal Lordship!

28

GLORY IN LISTENING

The Lord has given me a well-trained tongue that I might know how to speak to the weary a word that will rouse them. Morning after morning he opens my ear that I may hear.

(Is 50:4) (NAB)

THE ISRAELITES were in the desert for forty years. Jesus was in the desert for forty days. Both were in obedience to the Father's plan. The same mission was accomplished. The difference was in the listening.

In forty days Jesus was able to achieve what it took the Israelites forty years to achieve—listening and doing the Father's will.

The Father spoke these words to me:

I have the master plan
and I demand absolute obedience.
Obedient love.
Delayed obedience is disobedience.
You cannot afford to delay your obedience.
When I speak, I expect you to obey
with the simplicity of a child,
with the quickness of a child,
with the delight of a child who loves and trusts
His Father and knows the consequences for
disobedience or delayed obedience.

Father, You promised in Isaiah "morning after morning You open my ear that I may hear" (Is 50:4) (NAB). Not only open my ear to hear You, but empower me to be obedient to what I hear.

I ask the grace of absolute obedience, as Jesus had it. His whole life was in obedience to You. He spoke what You gave Him. He did what You showed Him. He was always about the Father's business.

Jesus, I, too, more than anything else desire to be about the Father's business. Empower me to discern what is for the Father's glory. Let the bottom line for all I do or not do be: Is my Father asking me to do this? If He isn't, no matter how good, how wonderful, how promising it is—if the Father is not asking me to do it, I will not be doing it.

29

YOURS THE POWER,
YOURS THE GLORY

Be sober and vigilant. Your opponent the devil is
prowling around like a roaring lion looking for
someone to devour. Resist him, steadfast in faith
knowing that your fellow believers throughout the
world undergo the same sufferings.

(1 Pt 5:8-9) (NAB)

I REMEMBER A BUSINESSMAN complaining to me, "The devil has
been nipping at my heels for several months just because the
Lord is calling me into His ministry."

"Do you say the Authority Prayer every day?" I asked.

"Well, I . . . say it sometimes," he hesitated.

Without hesitation, I stated: "The only reason the devil has
been nipping at your heels is because you have not crushed his
head with your heel. Don't you know that we have power to bind
his power?"

In the 1980s, this Authority Prayer was given by Jesus word
for word to a woman mystic in Canada. For the times in which
we are living, for the battle that is ongoing, Jesus exhorted that
we all pray it daily, even twice a day if you are in unusual war-
fare.

"In the name of Jesus, I take authority and I bind all the
powers and forces in the air, in the ground, in the water, in the
underground, in the netherworld, in nature, and in fire.

"You are the Lord over the entire universe, and I give You
the glory for Your creation. In Your name I bind all demonic
forces that have come against us and our families, and I seal all
of us in the protection of Your Precious Blood that was shed for
us on the cross. . . .

"Michael and our guardian angels, come and defend us and
our families in battle against all the evil ones that roam the earth.

"In the name of Jesus, I bind and command all the powers
and forces of evil to depart right now away from us, our homes

and our lands. And I thank you, Lord Jesus, for You are a faithful and compassionate God. Amen."

Pope John Paul has said, "Our greatest need after believing in and accepting a personal Savior is to believe in personified evil or a personal devil." Peter says: "Your opponent the devil is prowling around like a roaring lion looking for someone to devour" (1 Pt 5:8).

The devil is not about to devour us or even "nip at our heels" when in Jesus' name we have bound all his power—daily!

Numerous visionaries in the twentieth century have confirmed the revelation of Satan's 100-year reign in the twentieth century. According to some published accounts, Pope Leo XIII in 1884 experienced a terrible vision of demons and heard Satan in conversation with God. The demon reportedly boasted he could destroy the Church and seduce the world to hell if he were permitted the time and power. As the story goes, God granted Satan's request. And the twentieth century became the battlefield for the great confrontation. Lucifer was also given immense control over those who permitted themselves to be under his 'sign.' In response to the vision Pope Leo XIII composed the famous prayer to St. Michael the Archangel.

Two World Wars and millions of lives later, we now know that Pope Leo XIII's reported vision could not have been more accurate in its nature and content, especially with the rise of Communism, Revelations' Red Dragon.

Jesus, Lion of the tribe of Judah, protect us from all onslaughts of the evil one. Keep us faithful before we leave our bedrooms to daily pray the Authority Prayer that You have given us. You have won the battle by Your death and resurrection. We claim Your victory.

There is no question about who wins the battle. You won it for us almost two thousand years ago by the power of Your death and resurrection!

Jesus, You said, "All power is given to Me in heaven and on earth, as it is given to Me, so I give it to you!" Help us to believe in and to exercise Your power against the powers of darkness in our lives. Then without doubt Your Kingdom, Your Power and Your Glory will be ours forever and ever!

30

REVIVAL GLORY

And the glory of the Lord will be revealed, and all mankind together will see it. For the mouth of the Lord has spoken.

(Is 40:5)

"I AM WITH YOU. I have been with you. I will be with you.

"Fear not! I am doing a mighty work within you and through you. Do not despair of the darkness. Do not despair of the confusion. I am moving powerfully by the might of My Spirit.

"After the darkness and the confusion will come My light. The light of My glory will break through. You can trust Me for this. I am sovereignly moving by the power of My Spirit. Do not fear! My power is there to meet your need.

"As My people are praying, interceding, crying out for revival, I am preparing the world for a mighty revival in the power of My Holy Spirit. A revival in grace and glory like the world has never seen. As I said before: 'You have only scratched the surface for what I am ready to do!'

"Day by day, hour by hour, prayer by prayer, you are being readied! My people are being readied! My Church, My Bride is being readied for a mighty sovereign moving of My Spirit!

"It will come as sure as the ocean waves. It will move with a power like you have never seen before. This is My plan. It has been in the heart of My Father from all eternity. Nothing can thwart My plan. Nothing can stop My work.

"But you can expedite it. You can speed it up by being the instrument of My love, by preparing My people for the sovereign move of My Holy Spirit. You can speed it up, each time you cry out 'Maranatha! Come, Lord Jesus!'

"You are asking Me to come in the full power of My humanity and My divinity, in the full power of My miracles, My signs, My wonders. Even as I worked miracles throughout My lifetime in Galilee and Jerusalem, again I am working miracles and wonders in your cities and your nations. I am working with power in the lives of people all over the world.

"You are My disciple and I will use you as I used My apostles and My disciples. I will use you as I used Peter, Paul, James, John, Philip. As I used the holy women, Judith, Esther, Mary, Martha, and Mary Magdalene, I will use you in might and power. Through you I will call My people to a place of repentance, a place of healing, a place of anticipating a mighty sovereign moving of My spirit.

"I will use you as I prepare My bride, My Church, for My coming in power and in glory!"

Thank You, Lord Jesus, for that powerful word. I say Yes to Your prophetic word. Yes to all that You are doing in me and are about to do in the world through a mighty revival in the power of Your Holy Spirit. I say Yes to the sovereign moving of Your Holy Spirit planned from all eternity.

Maranatha! Come, Lord Jesus! Come!

With every beat of my heart, I cry out: Come, Lord Jesus! Come!

With every move of my body, I cry out: Come, Lord Jesus! Come!

With every step I take, I cry out: Come, Lord Jesus! Come!

With every word I speak, I cry out: Come, Lord Jesus! Come!

Maranatha! Come in glory!

31

GREATER THAN
THE HURRICANE GLORY

**Then Jesus said, "Did I not tell you that if you
believed, you would see the glory of God?"**

(Jn 11:40)

YESTERDAY WAS A DAY OF MIRACLES, the greatest of which was holding back the power of the hurricane threatening for days to hit Hawaii's North Shore by Sunday night! As I took the bus to Mass, colossal waves slashed the shore bathing our bus in ocean froth. As Sunday went on, we were warned to have a bag packed so that at a moment's notice the Army could evacuate us before midnight when the hurricane was predicted to hit.

I had never been near a tornado, much less a hurricane, so nothing within me was prepared for the massive wave of destruction preparing to hit my Kamehameha Prayer Pantry.

Like the Apostles in the boat on the stormy Sea of Galilee, my best bet was to keep my eyes on Jesus. I knew Peter's prayer: "Save us, O Lord, we are perishing" (Mt 8:25) (NAB). I prayed it often, especially just before retiring.

Close to midnight I stood facing the raging waters with my pyx and cross in hand, I prayed: "Jesus, when Clare of Assisi held up the Eucharist, the Saracens fell back! When You held up Your hand over the raging Sea of Galilee, the storm ceased! You are the same yesterday, today and forever! **In Your Name, Jesus,** I command the raging hurricane to stand still right now! Thank You, Jesus, for taking care of this. And Jesus, I do not have a radio, so do have someone phone me in the morning to tell me what You did."

With praise and thanks in my heart, it did not take me long to fall fast asleep. About 7:00 a.m. I was awakened when the phone rang. It was my friends, the Kennedys, from the mainland eager to tell me what happened to the hurricane.

For days, the hurricane had been advancing toward the North Shore with winds of seventy-five miles and more per hour.

Just before midnight, according to the weatherman's report, the hurricane like a Cyclops suddenly stood still in the middle of the ocean. Weathermen watched for a full hour not knowing what was happening, knowing only what had been predicted. Then defying any natural meteorological explanation, the hurricane made a 90 degree turn and dissolved in the ocean.

My 'Kamehameha Prayer Pantry' was spared! Praises went up not just from Oahu, but from friends across the U.S.A. who had been praying for my safety and protecting my time and space to write.

What a time to sing:
"Here comes Jesus. See Him walking on the water.
"He's the Master of the WAVES THAT ROLL . . . ."

Jesus, we are in awe of Your power to stop not just the hurricanes in the ocean but the storms in our lives. Thank you for all the times that You have been with us in miracle-working power saying "Peace! Be still!" to our storms.

Jesus, You are the Master of the "waves that will roll" into my life this day. Keep me calm in the storm trusting in Your divine direction and protection. Protect us from all that would destroy our families, our churches, our communities, our nations! Be with us in miracle power in the stormy days ahead.

32

THINE THE GLORY

Amen! Praise and glory and wisdom and thanks and honor and power and strength be to our God for ever and ever. Amen.

(Rv 7:12) (NRS)

FOR SUCH SOVEREIGN PROTECTION from the raging hurricane, I spent the entire day in pure thanksgiving for so great a miracle. Jesus spoke these words for you and for me: "As I used your prayers of intercession last night to hold back the power of the hurricane, so I use your prayers to hold back the hurricane of darkness, the deceit of sin that is being deluged upon the world. You, My people, have power in My name to stand up in authority against the Powers of Darkness. You have power to stand up against the forces that would destroy. I send you to 'proclaim liberty to the captives, and release to the prisoners.' I send you with power to bind those powers that would bring harm to My church or to My people. You will stand like oaks of justice planted by My own hand to show My glory."

"The Spirit of the Lord is upon me,
    because the Lord has anointed me;
He has sent me to bring glad tidings to the lowly,
    to heal the brokenhearted.
To proclaim liberty to the captives
    and release to the prisoners,
To announce a year of favor from the Lord
    and a day of vindication by our God,
    to comfort all who mourn;
To give them oil of gladness in place of mourning,
    a glorious mantle instead of a listless spirit.
They will be called oaks of justice,
    planted by the Lord to show his glory"
(Is 61:1-3) (NAB).

Jesus, You gave us power to bind the Powers of Darkness, that would threaten to destroy us. It was the last thing You did before You returned to Your Father in Heaven. You gave us power!

"These signs will follow those who believe. In My Name you will cast out demons. . . ." Let us not neglect this power that You gave us so Your Kingdom may come and the gates of hell shall not prevail against it.

This is a year of favor from the Lord, a day of vindication, clearance and pardon for all who ask it.

Father, we ask it: favor, vindication, clearance, pardon in Jesus' name for ourselves, our families, churches, cities, and nations. Thank you for planting us as oaks of justice to show Your glory now and forever.

33

PROMISED LAND GLORY

On that very day the Lord said to Moses, 'Go up on Mount Nebo, here in Abarim Mountains {it is in the land of Moab facing Jericho}, and view the land of Canaan, which I am giving to the Israelites as their possession. Then you shall die on the mountain you have climbed, and shall be taken to your people, just as your brother Aaron died on Mount Hor and there was taken to his people; because both of you broke faith with me among the Israelites at the waters of Meribath-kadesh in the desert of Zin by failing to manifest my sanctity among the Israelites. You may indeed view the land at a distance, but you shall not enter that land which I am giving to the Israelites.'

(Dt 32:48-52) (NAB)

IN THE SCRIPTURE READING TODAY from Deuteronomy, the Lord brought Moses to the Promised Land. God let his eyes feast on the whole land, but said that he would never enter it because he broke faith with Him at the waters of Meribeth-kadesh. Even though Moses was an intimate friend of God, because he "failed to manifest God's sanctity among the Israelites" on one occasion, he was not allowed to enter the Promised Land.

"So there in the land of Moab, Moses, the servant of the Lord, died as the Lord had said. . . . Moses was one hundred twenty years old when he died, yet his eyes were undimmed, his vigor unabated" (Dt 34:5,7) (NAB). Who of us wouldn't love to have "eyes undimmed and vigor unabated?"

When I had my sixtieth birthday (half of what Moses lived, with his eyes undimmed and his vigor unabated), the Lord woke me in my sleep with this word: "I am going to renew your energies like those of a teenager."

I knew that by morning I would deny or question what I had heard, so I got up in the middle of the night and wrote: "I am going to renew your energies like those of a teenager!"

About a month later when I was having lunch with my friend, Rose, the confirmation came. As we were chatting, Rose startled me with "I can't get over it, Sister Fran! You have the energies of a teenager!"

Lord God of Israel, in this time when many are looking to all sorts of energizers for renewed energies, help us to come to You first for the help we need. You are the great I Am. Let us hear You say to us: "I am the source. I am the beginning, the end and all the in-betweens of all that you need. I am Eternal Life! I am the energy that you need to sustain you. I am the healing that you need to claim. Look to My love and to My promises. What is impossible for you is very possible for Me."

I hear Your voice, O God, and I say Yes not only to what You would do but to the way that You would do it!

Lord, God of Israel, in spite of the many times that we have broken faith with You, bring all whom we love to repentance so that we may all be with You forever in Your heavenly Promised Land.

34

GOD OF GLORY THUNDERS

The voice of the Lord is over the waters; the God of glory thunders, the Lord thunders over the mighty waters.

(Ps 29:3)

IN THE PSALMS I found words for a listening heart. More and more I understand, it is not the writing; it is the receiving, the listening. Today was the last of seven days for preparing my vessel to receive. It was my deepest experience of knowing what a vast empty vessel I am to receive whatever God would pour into me. My desire was to be obedient. Like Mary I prayed: "Be it done to me according to Your word."

I stood in the place of need, with a total inability to move forward in that need. The day was spent in yielding my whole being, imagination, understanding, mind, heart, and will to God's purpose on a deeper and deeper level.

I was reminded of my bedroom "prayer pantry" back in Milwaukee. Across the doorway I have a Yield sign to remind me daily to yield to the Father, the Son, and the Holy Spirit. The more I yield, the more I receive. The more I am emptied, the more I will be filled.

"You have turned my mourning into dancing; you have taken off my sackcloth and clothed me with joy, that my heart may praise you and not be silent. O Lord, my God, I will give thanks to you forever" (Ps 30:11-12) (NRS).

"I have seen you in the sanctuary and beheld your power and your glory" (Ps 63:2).

Father, Jesus, Holy Spirit, it is up to You. There is nothing I can do to make things happen. I am in Your hands. I open my hands and heart to receive all that You would give for Your people and for myself.

"They that wait upon the Lord shall renew their strength. They shall mount up with wings like an eagle" (Is 40:31) (NRS).

I wait upon You, O God, in the Pantry of Your Divine Stillness for every word, every understanding, every phrase. Renew my strength today that I may soar with wings like an eagle.

35

STILL BEFORE THE GLORY

**So I got up and went out to the plain. And the glory
of the Lord was standing there, like the glory I had
seen by the Kebar River, and I fell facedown.**

(Ez 3:23)

"I CAN BEST TEACH YOU when you are truly humble before Me. The
enemy is best thwarted when you are poured out in adoration
before Me."

As God's people were in rebellion again and again, there
were seasons when Moses was on his face before God for forty
days and forty nights without eating.

To be on my face before God poured out in adoration is
often the call that is my prayer life.

"I would have you be faithful to that call as the prophets
were faithful. I can only use you when you are little and simple
before Me. When you get too big with ideas and plans of your
own I cannot use you. So let go of your need to have it all figured
out. I, your God, have it all figured out. I know exactly *what* I
want to do. I know exactly *how* I want to do it. I know exactly
when I want to do it. My timetable is perfect. As long as you
remain little, you will be perfectly on My timetable."

I am reminded of one of our elderly Sisters on a retreat with
us sharing about prostrating herself before the Lord in prayer. "I
always thought it was quite undignified and unnecessary until I
tried it. While I was prostrate, the Lord spoke: 'In that lowly posi-
tion before Me the enemy can't shoot holes through you. You are
safe.'"

*Father God, You are ever present in the whole world. You
hold the whole world in Your hands. Hold the whole of me
close to Your heart today. Protect me from the enemy who
"would sift me and have me."*

Jesus, pray for us the prayer You prayed for Your apostles the night before You died: "Father I want those you have given me to be with me where I am, and to see my glory, the glory you have given me because you loved me before the creation of the world" (Jn 17:24).

Jesus, we desire to see the glory that You have been given because the Father loved You before the creation of the world. We desire to see that glory that You have been given. We desire to be in that glory.

Prepare us for that glory. O yes, God, the Kingdom, the Power and the Glory is all there! The Kingdom, the Power and the Glory are Yours now and forever and ever. Amen.

36

REVIVAL GLORY

'I will shake all nations, and the desired of all nations will come, and I will fill this house with glory. The glory of this present house will be greater than the glory of the former house. And in this place I will grant peace,' declares the Lord Almighty.

(Hg 2:7,9)

DICKENS BEGINS HIS NOVEL *Tale of Two Cities* with "It was the best of times and the worst of times."

As we are moving with momentum toward the third millennium, this could well be a banner statement over the times that we are living in: "The best of times; and the worst of times."

It is certainly the best of times for what God is doing to pour out His Holy Spirit, His unfathomable mercy, and His measureless love across the face of the earth.

It is the best of times for, as Pope John Paul says, we are moving toward the time of fulfillment of all that God has promised, "a collapse in the power of evil and some great 'springtime' for Christianity and the world" (Pope John Paul II's Apostolic Letter, *With the Coming of the Third Millennium*).

It is the best of times for we have moved beyond the Renewal of Vatican II, even beyond the renewal of the Renewal. We are in a time for all Churches and all peoples to experience Revival.

I have seen revival in places as small as a fifty person Wednesday night prayer meeting and as large as a 2,500 person gathering in the Cathedral Church in Dominica, West Indies.

When the Presence of God is proclaimed to release the gift of tongues in 2,500 people in response to one teaching and the explosion of praise almost knocks the Vicar General over—that is Revival! When God's Presence is proclaimed to meet the need for deliverance from every demonic spirit and they leave—that is Revival! When Jesus in the Blessed Sacrament is carried in procession up and down the Cathedral aisles for an hour and a half

with a constant flow of the Word of Knowledge for healings—
that is Revival!

*O God, I say Yes to all that You are doing and wanting to do
across the face of the earth. It is the "best of times" for You to
move in the full power of Your Spirit in my heart, my mind,
and my spirit. I say Yes to all that You have done and Yes to
all that You desire to do.*

*Jesus, You are the eternal "Yes" to the Father. I join my "Yes"
to your "Yes" that the Father may be glorified in Your life
lived in me. We say "Yes" to whatever way You would use us
to do all that You did and greater things—that the Father
might be glorified in all.*

*Use us in miracle healing power that the blind may see, the
deaf may hear, the lame may walk, the "lepers" of our day
may be cleansed. "One sign, one wonder can do more for the
Kingdom than a whole shelf of theology books!"*

*Let our lives be an answer to Pope John's prayer: "Renew
Your wonders in this our day as with a new Pentecost."*

*True we are living in the best of times and the worst of times.
And true like in the early Church "our present sufferings are
not worth comparing with the glory that will be revealed in
us" (Rom 8:18).*

*Revival, let it come, O Lord! First in my own heart, family,
community, church, nation, and then let the fires of revival
burn in the nations of the world!*

37

ALL FOR THE GLORY OF GOD

**So whether you eat or drink or whatever you do, do it
all for the glory of God.**

(1 Cor 10:31)

FRIDAY, THE 13TH, was anything but a Friday the 13th!

It was a good day, a quiet day with a call to get more and
more quiet under the healing power of God in the healing presence of the Father, Son, and the Holy Spirit. Whenever I have had
one, two, or three months alone and away for writing, I have
been in the habit of setting three extra places at the table for my
evening meal. One for the Father, one for the Son, and one for the
Holy Spirit. The Father's place had flowers or something beautiful from creation, Jesus' place, the Scripture opened, and the Holy
Spirit, a lit candle.

The first time I did this, after being in the awesome
Presence for a long, long time, I was about to get up when the
Father stopped me with: "You haven't asked permission."

At every evening meal from that night on, before leaving
the table, I would pause to ask, "Father, do You have anything to
say? Jesus, do You have anything to say? Holy Spirit, do You
have anything to say?"

God is as close to us as our next thought. When that
thought comes in the first person, it can be God speaking. When
I left my prayer spot in Pinellas Park, Florida, after two months
of prayer, I had eight tapes filled with God speaking.

One meal I began with: "Speak, Lord, Your servant is listening." Quickly, I heard: "Speak, Fran, your God is listening."

*Speak, Lord, I desire to hear Your still small voice affirming
me in my walk and talk with You. Speak words of love,
forgiveness and healing. I am all Yours, You are all mine.*

I say yes to Your mighty irresistible love sovereignly moving in my heart this day. Yes to Your Holy Spirit sovereignly cleansing my mind from all that is not of You. Yes to Your Holy Spirit moving in and renewing my spirit.

Glorious God, whether we eat or drink or whatever we do, we are challenged by You to do it all for Your glory. Be present to us today, especially during our meals. Let us know that You are the Silent Guest listening to every conversation.

Prepare us for that eternal Banquet Feast with You in heaven where we will join the great multitude singing: "Hallelujah! Salvation and glory and power and might belong to our God, for true and just are his judgments" (Rv 19:1) (NAB).

"Let us rejoice and be glad and give him glory! For the wedding of the Lamb has come, and his bride has made herself ready. Fine linen, bright and clean, was given her to wear. Then the angel said to me, 'Write this: 'Blessed are those who are invited to the wedding supper of the Lamb!' The angel continued, 'These are the true words of God'" (Rv 19:7-9).

38

VOICE OF GLORY

Give to the Lord glory and praise. Give to the Lord the glory due his name. Adore the Lord in holy attire. The voice of the Lord is over the waters. The God of glory thunders. O ye mighty, give unto the Lord glory. The voice of the Lord is mighty, the voice of the Lord is majestic. The voice of the Lord twists the oaks and strips the forests, And in his temple all say: "Glory!"

(Ps 29:1-4,9) (NAB)

ALLOW AND INVITE the words of Psalm 29 to get to your spiritual gut today. Your hearts will be filled with glory and praise. Not just once but many times over. "O ye mighty, give unto the Lord glory." We may not feel mighty, but the fact of our giving unto the Lord glory lifts us up above all that would weigh us down.

How glibly over the years have we concluded our psalms and other prayers with the Great Doxology, "Glory be to the Father, and to the Son, and to the Holy Spirit; as it was in the beginning is now and forever, world without end. Amen!" Today let us have a new sense of awe, enthusiasm, and excitement as we pray "Glory be to the Father, and to the Son, and to the Holy Spirit!" If theirs is the Kingdom, the Power and the Glory, then we can let go of our "fallen" need for glory, for a kingdom here, for power here, for glory here. "Thine is the Kingdom, the Power, the Glory, forever and ever. Amen."

In 1971 when I was about to go into prison ministry at a Federal Correction Institute in Milan, Michigan, the Lord spoke: "Your only problems will be to believe what I am ready to do and to get in My way by claiming the glory."

Every Friday night before we went out for our Saturday ministry in prison, we spent several hours praising God for what He would do the next day and binding all the Powers of Darkness that would attempt to prevent God's working. In our year's ministry, I can't recall one prisoner we prayed for whom God did not physically heal or set free emotionally or spiritually.

I will never forget the day we prayed for a professed Satanist who had a litany of sin that would make a bestseller. He wanted prayer for his twin brother whom he had led into Satanism. The brother was dying from a tumor on the brain. Would we pray for him for healing?

My first thought was: "Man, you've got more faith than I have. But if you have the faith, God has the power."

"Allow us to pray with you first to accept Jesus as your Savior and Your Baptizer in the Holy Spirit," I suggested. "Then together we can pray for your twin brother's healing." He did and we did.

When we returned the next week this young man stood at the gate glowing with the Glory of God and the Good News. "My brother is healed! Healed! Healed! Here is a letter from him. The tumor is gone! He is healed. My whole life is changed. God is real! Jesus is real!"

When Jesus went through the villages He healed everyone. When Jesus went through the prison He healed everyone who asked. My book, *Wow, God* has a few of the many stories that could be told.

God will share His glory with no one. I like to recall the time I prayed for a Sister friend who rested in the Spirit. Later she shared a vision of a huge magnificent mosaic lit up in only a few places.

"Why," she asked the Lord, "is it lit up in only a few places?" The Lord replied, "The places that are lit up are the few times that you gave Me all the glory for what I have done in your life, and for ways that I have used you for other people's lives."

O God, we give You permission to meet us where we are in the place of our lowliness and our inordinate need to share in Your glory.

For all that You have done in our lives and for all the ways that You have used us for others, O God we give You all the glory! All the glory is due Your Name. Glory be to God the Father, glory be to God the Son, and glory be to God the Holy Spirit. Let our glory be—to be without glory—that all glory, honor, and praise may be Yours, Holy God, forever and ever. Amen.

39

GLORY OF THE RESURRECTION

All of us, gazing on the Lord's glory with unveiled faces, are being transformed from glory to glory into his very image by the Lord who is the Spirit.

(2 Cor 3:18) (NAB)

FROM GLORY TO GLORY He is changing us. We have only begun to receive that change. As I was reading *Restoring the Christian Soul through Healing Prayer* by Leanne Payne, I became aware of the need to get rid of all negativity in my life. In other words, to undergo more "changing."

Quieting myself in prayer one day, the Lord led me to see all the ways that I do not like myself. Like a late, late show, the pictures and script were visible, bringing into the light every negative experience of my life that I might bring them one by one to the foot of the cross.

Nothing can change us so much as time spent at the foot of the cross, claiming not just the graces of Calvary but the full power and glory of the Resurrection. It was a "Garbage to Glory" experience like I had never known before. On an entirely new level, I knew the truth Paul speaks of when he says: "I live now not I, but Christ lives in me." The Father, Son, and Holy Spirit have their abode in me.

Father, Son, and Holy Spirit, I thank You for Your indwelling Presence all these years. Forgive me my neglect and lack of awareness of Your holy presence within me. Teach me by Your Spirit to allow that great mystery of Your presence within me to become the life of my life and the power that will transform me into Your likeness with ever-increasing glory.

40

EVER-INCREASING GLORY

**You changed my mourning into dancing; you took off
my sackcloth and clothed me with gladness that my
soul might sing praise to you without ceasing; O Lord,
my God, forever will I give you thanks.**

(Ps 30:12-13) (NAB)

EVERY DAY I AIM TO PRAY in my prayer language at least fifteen to
thirty minutes for an increase and a release of all the gifts, all the
power and all the fruit of the Holy Spirit. People sometimes ask
me, "If you are filled with the Holy Spirit, why would you ask for
more. Do you leak?"

Leak? No! However, "if our output is greater than our
input, we go 'kaput!'"

If we want to "sing praise to our God without ceasing" and
minister to God's glory "without counting the cost" we need a lot
of power poured in so a lot of power can be poured out.

"O, Lord, my God forever will I give you thanks that my
soul might sing to you without ceasing." There were days when
there were not enough seconds to the minute and minutes to the
hour to receive and give thanks for all the ways that God wanted to share of His glory.

The glory of the King's son or daughter is within. To sit in
His Presence and bask in His glory left no room for viewing the
"boob tube" or even checking the radio for what was happening
in the world.

My world was: "All of us, gazing on the Lord's glory with
unveiled faces, are being transformed from glory to glory into his
very image by the Lord who is the Spirit" (2 Cor 3:18) (NAB).

"If the ministry that condemns men is glorious, how much
more glorious is the ministry that brings righteousness! For what
was glorious has no glory now in comparison with the surpassing glory" (2 Cor 3:9-10) (NIV).

Yes, God, You have changed my mourning into dancing. You have clothed me with gladness that I might sing praise to You without ceasing.

Day by day, I am being transformed into Your likeness with ever-increasing glory which comes from You, Lord Jesus. Today I am way down the road from where I was yesterday. I am way down the road from where I was last week. But I am not yet where I will be tomorrow, next week, or next year.

"Indeed the glory that once was is no glory at all; it is outshone by a still greater glory" (2 Cor 3:10) (NEB). Seal the glory in me with Your Precious Blood that in no way may I be robbed by the enemy.

"Then your light will break forth like the dawn, and your wound shall quickly be healed; your vindication shall go before you, and the glory of the Lord shall be your rear guard" (Is 58:8) (NAB).

41

GLORY OF JUSTICE

Grace is poured out on your lips. Thus God blessed you forever . . . in your splendor and your majesty. In your glory and your splendor ride on triumphant. In the cause of truth and for the sake of justice may your right hand show your wondrous deeds.

(Ps 45:3,5) (NAB)

THIS IS A WORD and a power I claim today. Show us the work of justice. Therefore shall nations "praise you forever for you shall make them princes through all the land" (Ps 45:18) (NAB).

Here is a thought for today from a Founding Father, Thomas Jefferson: "God who gave us life gave us liberty. Can the liberties of a nation be secure when we have removed a conviction that these liberties are a gift of God? Indeed I tremble for my country when I reflect that God is just, and that His justice cannot sleep forever."

"You love justice and hate wickedness. Therefore your God has anointed you with the oil of gladness above your fellow kings" (Ps 45:8) (NAB).

In 1982 with five thousand Christians, I was part of "Washington for Jesus," a day of prayer from sunrise to sunset on the Mall. One speaker shared that without conversion, he would give our nation at the most ten years to be destroyed on any one of three counts: moral corruption, financial ruin, or outside conquest.

Today in 1998 as we evaluate the world scene as pictured and written about in issues of *Time, Newsweek* and *U.S. News and World Report*, we might well believe that barring the miracle power and mercy of God this word could well describe the fate of our nation in the new millennium.

You have done it, O God, and You are doing it. Anoint me afresh this day with the oil of gladness for works of justice! Whatever it is that I am called to do, let Your anointing fall on me that I may serve the works of justice with joy and with gladness.

Awaken our nation and the nations of the world to works of justice and to correct all that is injustice. In the Name of Jesus, with the Blood of Jesus, with the Word of Jesus, I free all lawmakers to think new thoughts and to feel new feelings regarding works of truth and justice. By Your Spirit, empower our lawmakers to work in the cause of truth and for the sake of justice.

42

ETERNAL WEALTH OF GLORY

**Fear not when a man grows rich when the wealth of
his house becomes great, for when he dies he shall
take none of it. His glory shall not follow him down.
Though in his lifetime he counted himself blessed.**

(Ps 49:17-19) (NAB)

THE STORY IS TOLD of a Christian man who had accumulated great
wealth. The words from Psalm 49 were very clear to him. "When
he dies he shall take none of it. His wealth shall not follow him."

If only he could take with him something of his vast riches,
he would be content. He finally found one preacher who said:
"You can take just one small case."

Instantly he knew what he would do! Take one small case
lined with bricks of gold!

He died. Arrived at the gate, case in hand. The order was
given: "Open it up."

Glory! There were the rows of gold bricks. Peter shook his
head. "Sir, I realize that you were a very rich man, and I can
appreciate that you would want to take something of your riches
with you as you enter into glory. But why would you bring pavement?"

*In Your Word, Lord, You remind us "How deep are the
riches, the wisdom and the knowledge of God" (Rom 11:33)
(NAB).*

*When we grow rich in the things of God, not only will the
riches and the glory be with us here on earth but they will
follow us into eternity. This is what today's living is about!
Riches! Eternal riches! Glory! Eternal glory!*

All is passing save to love God and serve Him alone. Then that eternal weight of riches and glory will be ours forever and ever.

"May he enlighten your innermost vision that you may know the great hope to which he has called you, the wealth of his glorious heritage to be distributed among the members of the church, and the immeasurable scope of his power in us who believe. It is like the strength he showed in raising Christ from the dead and seating him at his right hand in heaven" (Eph 1:18-20) (NAB).

43

THE GLORY OF SURRENDER

**O God, you are my God whom I seek; for you my
flesh pines, my soul thirsts, like the earth parched,
lifeless and without water. Thus have I gazed towards
you in the sanctuary to see your power and your glory.
For your kindness is a greater good than life; my lips
glorify you.**

(Ps 63:2-4) (NAB)

AGAIN FOR ME the sanctuary of His Presence was that majestic
Pacific. As I went down for an hour on the ocean front, it became
for me a mammoth sanctuary. I would kneel on the ocean floor,
sign myself with the Cross and let the glory of the waves sweep
over me again and again as I burst forth in the praises of my
prayer language!

"Thus have I gazed towards You in the sanctuary to see
Your power and Your glory." As the waves swept over me, the
power and the glory swept over me again and again. To kneel in
that holy place was to experience the power and the glory.

"Ascribe to the Lord the glory due his name; worship the
Lord in the splendor of his holiness" (Ps 29:2).

"The voice of the Lord is over the waters; the God of glory
thunders, the Lord thunders over the mighty waters" (Ps 29:3).

"Shout joyfully to God all you on earth. Sing praise to the
glory of His name. Proclaim God's glorious praise" (Ps 66:2)
(NAB).

From wherever we are, we are invited today to shout joyfully to God together with all the rest of the earth. We are invited
in the three-thousand-year-old prayers of King David "to sing
praise to the glory of God's name and proclaim His glorious
praise."

This is holy ground, O God! Wherever I am! I am aware of Your awesome Presence! I cry out: "You are my God whom I seek in this place. For You my flesh yearns, my soul thirsts. Like a dry land parched and devoid of waste so I have longed to see You and behold Your power and Your glory."

Today may not have an ocean floor in sight, but whatever the floor, I desire it to become a place where I can pour out my life in worship and in praise. So I do pour out my life like the alabaster jar of Mary Magdalene. No stock market floor has such rich returns as the sanctuary of Your praises. 100% of me surrendered to You yields 100% of You surrendered to me. That is profit!

44

EXCHANGE THE GLORY

They exchanged their glory for the image of grass eating bulls. They forgot the God who had saved them, who had done great deeds in Egypt.

(Ps 106:20) (NAB)

IT IS SO EASY TO FORGET the God who has saved us and to allow our lives to pile up a lot of Christian or non-Christian clutter.

We actually exchange the glory that is on us maybe not for images of "grass eating bulls" but for images of just plain "stuff."

Rummage sales are the Number Two sport of the nation according to a recent Milwaukee Star Journal report. The question is: "Do we own our trappings or do they own us?"

So we spend a lifetime accumulating stuff. And what happens to it? All the one-time treasures will soon be someone else's stuff. We can use hundreds of words to describe the things that fill our lives and our homes, but they can all be summed up in one small word: "Stuff!"

A couple of summers ago at a Texas Bible Institute talent show, just for fun I decided to do my own Christian version of George Carlin's dramatic monologue on "stuff."

I had asked the Lord for a beginning, an ending, and something in-between. According to the audience, God gave me a stellar performance ending with: "Tell everyone whoever gives up all their 'stuff' for the Kingdom that He will give you back a hundredfold in this life and forever in the next."

God calls us today to a time of repentance for the times that we exchanged His glory for our "stuff," for anything less than Him.

Father, Son, and Holy Spirit, You alone know how often I have exchanged Your glory for "stuff" that I put in place of an ever-deepening, growing relationship with You! Forgive Me.

Quicken My awareness when I am making unwise choices. Lead me by Your Spirit to let go of "stuff" I no longer need.

My goal is for eternal riches, "stuff" that rust will not corrode nor moth consume.

45

REIGN OF GLORY

May the whole earth be filled with his glory.

(Ps 72:19) (NAB)

IN THE BOOK OF GENESIS when the Spirit moved over the waters He brought order out of chaos. By the power of the Holy Spirit I pray that all that is chaotic in nature as well as in peoples be brought back to Divine Order. I pray that the power of God's Holy Spirit move miraculously across the face of the earth, that every continent, country, nation be visited by the Spirit of God.

May the nations of the world be helped because of the glory of Your name, O Lord God of Hosts. May the power of the Powers of Darkness be forever broken and Your glory reign over all the earth! For the Kingdom, the Power and the Glory are Yours forever!

"Help us O God, our Savior because of the glory of your name. Why should the nations say 'Where is their God?'" (Ps 79) (NAB).

"Whoever is begotten by God conquers the world. And the victory that conquers the world is our faith. Who (indeed) is the victor over the world but the one who believes that Jesus is the Son of God?" (1 Jn 5:4-5) (NAB).

We believe that You, Father God, do move miraculously among the nations for the glory of Your name. We believe You reveal to them the truth about Who Jesus is. "Whoever is begotten of God conquers the world." We believe You raise up godly politicians so that the world may be conquered for God.

We pray today "In the Name of Jesus, by the Blood of Jesus, by the Word of Jesus, we free all politicians to think new thoughts and feel new feelings. And we free all people to think new thoughts and to feel new feelings about electing godly politicians and world leaders."

CREDIT THE GLORY

Ascribe to the Lord, O heavenly beings, ascribe to the Lord glory and strength. Ascribe to the Lord the glory due his name; worship the Lord in holy splendor. The voice of the Lord is over the waters; the God of glory thunders, the Lord, over mighty waters. The voice of the Lord causes the oaks to whirl, and strips the forest bare; and in his temple all say, 'Glory!'

(Ps 29:1-3,9) (NRS)

ASCRIBE MEANS WE ARE TO GIVE, to assign, to attribute, to credit the Lord the glory due His name.

This is an assignment from the Living God for us today—to credit the Lord with glory and strength. As we do we can know that He will be there in glory and strength for us no matter how great our need.

"Ascribe to the Lord the glory due his name" (Ps 29:2). Glory is due today from our lips, from our heart, from our whole being, to the God of glory, to the name of Yahweh, Father, Son, and Holy Spirit. We are called to worship, to pour out our lives in the splendor of His holiness.

If nothing else happened in our entire day this would make life worth living.

Teach us, O loving and eternal God, how to give to You the glory due to Your name. Teach us how to guard against sneaking some of the glory for our own name. Teach us as You taught King David to be forever caught up in proclaiming evermore Your glory.

You are a God of glory and strength. You will be there for me no matter how great is my need. I ascribe to You all glory and strength! I will not be lacking in strength today for I can lean on Your strength. In Your temple all say GLORY! I unite today with all the voices that thunder over the waters, and twist the oaks and say GLORY! I give you the GLORY due Your name.

47

TOWERS OF GLORY

**I will give thanks to you, O Lord, among the peoples.
I will chant your praise among the nations. For your
kindness towers to the heavens, and your faithfulness
to the skies. Be exalted above the heavens, O God;
above all the earth be your glory.**

(Ps 57:9-12) (NAB)

A FAVORITE HYMN in the Renewal across the world is from Psalm 57. "For your kindness towers to the heavens, and your faithfulness to the skies" (Ps 57:11) (NAB).

I have been in stadiums where forty thousand voices exploded in song: "Your kindness towers to the heavens and Your faithfulness to the skies." What an encouraging thought! I can expect "God's kindness in my life today to tower to the heavens and His faithfulness to the skies."

As the notes soar above the heavens we know something is happening in the heavens that has its roots on earth. And something is happening on earth that is reverberated throughout the heavens.

In the hearts of people among all nations, we are proclaiming that our God be exalted above the heavens and His glory be over all the earth. As His glory spills out we in turn are given a great feeling of joy, pride, and power in our God.

Today is a day to look for God's glory to explode over our little or big corner of the earth. We can know that God's glory is there because we have prayed that His glory be over all the earth. In our spirit we can see it coming on the wings of the wind. God's glory moving like a mighty wind leaving in its trail: blessings, healings, miracles!

Glory be to the Father, and to the Son, and to the Holy Spirit, as it was in the beginning, is now and forever, world without end. Amen. I make the Great Doxology my prayer today. God, I let go of my need for glory so that Your glory may come down and flood my life. Flood the earth with Your glory, O God.

O, God, You can never be outdone in kindness. Your kindness towers to the heavens and Your faithfulness to the skies.

48

WORKS OF GLORY

Let your works be seen by your servants and your glory by their children. May the gracious care of the Lord our God be ours. Prosper the work of our hands.

(Ps 90:16-17) (NAB)

OVER THE YEARS I heard the story told of an elderly woman who had raised a family and been a true servant of God in the larger community she lived in. Retired, she would spend long hours of prayer in the church. When asked what prayers she prayed, she responded simply: "I don't say anything. I just show God my hands."

As we sit today in the stillness of our prayer pantry, let us offer our God all the work of our hands!

In the words of the Psalmist, let us ask God to "prosper the work of our hands."

In the words of Johnny Cash, "Put your hand in the Hand of the Man who stilled the waters. Put your hand in the Hand of the Man from Galilee."

Yes God, receive again the work of our hands from years of service. Forgive what needs to be forgiven. Bless and prosper the work of our hands as today they work to do Your will.

Use our hands this day for the healing of Your people. You promised "these signs will accompany those who believe. In My name you will place your hands on the sick and they will get well" (Mk 16:18). Prosper the work of our hands and bless the hands of those we serve.

Teach us evermore how to walk with You as we walk, to talk with You as we talk, and to live as though the Kingdom had come today.

That all the troubled waters of my life may be quieted, I choose today to "put my hand in the Hand of the Man from Galilee."

49

NEW SONGS OF GLORY

Sing to the Lord a new song; sing to the Lord, all you lands. Sing to the Lord, bless his name; announce his salvation day after day. Tell his glory among the nations; among all people, his wondrous deeds. Give to the Lord, you families of nations, give to the Lord glory and praise; give to the Lord the glory due His name.

(Ps 96:1-3,7) (NAB)

"SING TO THE LORD a new song." That means a song no one has ever sung! A song no one has ever heard! Sing it to the Lord! Tell His glory among the nations with a new harmony, a new melody, new words that no one has ever heard!

That is an invitation from God's word for all of us today no matter how gifted or ungifted we are in music and voice.

Dr. Wiewel, a ninety-year-old doctor (still practicing her osteopathic skills) visited me one day. She had read *Wow, God* and was intrigued with the possibility of receiving all the gifts of the Holy Spirit, especially the gift of tongues. We prayed. She received.

Weeks later Dr. Wiewel wrote to me sharing the marvelous changes in her life. One that left her in utter amazement was the fact that for the first time in her ninety years, she found herself singing around the house in English and in other tongues.

"Sing to the Lord a new song." At age ninety, she was singing new songs with countless variations. WOW! WOW means we are <u>wi</u>th<u>ou</u>t <u>w</u>ords for what God is doing.

Several years ago as I was praying with Father Jack McGinnis at an ACT Conference, I received this word. "There are many songs in the Heart of the Father that no one has ever sung. He wants to give you one."

The next morning Jack sang out a song in the Spirit recorded on a tape entitled "The Carpenter."

"You are the carpenter, I am the wood.
You are the carpenter, I am the wood.
I am the carpenter, you are the wood.
I am the carpenter, you are the wood.
I am the carpenter, you are my wood.
I am the carpenter, you are my wood.
I am. You are."

Today Father God, I, too, desire to delight Your heart with a new song that no one has ever sung. Not just one for today, but a new song every day for the rest of my life. In the power of Your Spirit, enable me to sing many new songs, many melodies that will resound to Your glory and praise for all eternity.

50

KISWAHILI GLORY

Let all the earth acclaim God. Sing to the glory of his name. Make his praise glorious. Say to God 'How awesome are your deeds; Your foes cower before the greatness of your strength. The whole world bows low in your presence. They praise your name in song.'

(Ps 66:1-4) (REB)

ON ONE OF OUR INTERCESSION RETREATS some years ago, we thought we had exhausted the lists of all those for whom we were called to intercede. Then we received: "Ask of Me, and I will make the nations your heritage, and the ends of the earth your possession" (Ps 2:8) (NAB).

"Lord, we are asking," we prayed.

As we would lift up nation after nation in our prayer language, Germany, France, Russia, Africa, Japan, Israel, God would give us the language of each nation. When we prayed for Africa, the Kiswahili sounds were so real you could almost hear the African drums in the background.

Father, Son, and Holy Spirit, enlarge our hearts this day to take in all the nations of the world. Give us the "nations for our inheritance and the ends of the earth for our possession."

You, Jesus, lived, died, rose in glory and have been living for almost two thousand years to make intercession for all the nations of the earth. Yet 4.7 billion people still await Your full message. Give to us, O Lord, and to Your Church a missionary heart, a missionary mind and a missionary spirit. Let nothing be too much to give that Your Kingdom may reach the ends of the earth. Let Your full glory come on earth as it is in heaven!

51

WINDS OF GLORY

**Bless the Lord, O my soul! O Lord, my God, you are
great indeed! You are clothed with majesty and glory,
robed in light as with a cloak. You have spread out the
heavens like a tent cloth, you have constructed your
palace upon waters. You make the clouds your chariot,
you travel on the wings of the wind.**

(Ps 104:1-4) (NAB)

TODAY WAS A SPECIAL DAY for experiencing the winds in nature and
in the Word. From Genesis through Revelation, *wind* appears
more than one hundred times.

"So God made a wind sweep over the earth and the waters
began to subside" (Gn 8:1) (NAB).

"There arose a wind sent by the Lord, that drove in quail
from the sea and brought them down over the campsite at a
height of two cubits from the ground for the distance of a day's
journey all around the camp" (Nm 11:31) (NAB).

After David's exploits with the Philistines, he sings about
being borne on the wings of the wind. "He mounted a cherub and
flew, borne on the wings of the wind" (2 Samuel 22:11).

Jesus commanded the wind on the Sea of Galilee. "He woke
up, rebuked the wind, and said to the sea: 'Quiet! Be still!' The
wind ceased and there was great calm. Then he asked them,
'Why are you so terrified? Do you not yet have faith?' They were
filled with great awe and said to one another: 'Who then is this
whom even wind and the sea obey?'" (Mk 4:39-41) (NAB).

Jesus sent forth His spirit with the sound of a mighty wind.
"Suddenly from up in the sky there came a noise like a strong,
driving wind which was heard all through the house where they
were seated" (Acts 2:2) (NAB).

Yahweh, "You are clothed with majesty and glory, robed in light as with a cloak. You have spread out the heavens like a tent cloth. You have constructed Your palace upon the waters. You make the clouds Your chariot. You travel on the wings of the wind." All of nature is in Your control.

Creator God, give to us a new reverence and awe for all the forces of nature. Like Francis, give us a heart to bless again and again all the elements of nature: Brother Sun and Sister Moon that they may lead us to a deeper and deeper awe of You as our Creator God, and sustainer of the universe. Our security is in Your Presence and Your promises. You are a faithful God. Make of us a faithful people.

52

DREAMS OF GLORY

And the Word became flesh and made his dwelling among us, and we saw his glory, the glory of the Father's only Son full of grace and of truth.

(Jn 1:14) (NAB)

WE HAVE SEEN GOD'S GLORY and we will continue to see His glory in our own hearts and in the hearts of all He has given us to love. We have seen it! It is real! It will continue to become more and more real until He comes in glory.

We can become vessels of that "enduring love" to be poured out until He comes in glory. The moments when the Shekinah Glory, God's visible manifestation of majesty in power, flooded my room became more and more frequent.

One day out of the quiet I received this word: My glory is upon you. My glory is around you. My glory is above and below you. You are filled with My glory. Even though you do not understand it, I ask that you accept it. Allow yourself to be bathed in My glory, clothed in My glory, endued with My glory.

This is not something you are called to program. What is happening today has been programmed by My Spirit from all eternity. There is nothing you can do to add to My glory. My glory is infinite beyond limit and beyond understanding. I share My glory with you; it is not you sharing Your glory with Me. A perfect prayer for you will always be: "Glory be to the Father, and to the Son, and to the Holy Spirit, as it was in the beginning is now and forever. Amen."

"Of His fullness we have all had a share" (Jn 1:16). But nothing compared to what is to come soon and very soon! While we await His coming, it is ours to dream dreams about what it will be like when He comes in glory.

One night at an international, interdenominational Feast of Tabernacles conference in Jerusalem, the theme was "Rehearsal for the Wedding Feast of the Lamb." Everyone was encouraged to come dressed in white. Women came with flowers in their hair and men with boutonnieres. Musicians led us in songs of the Bride and Bridegroom, while dancers in choreography carried out the theme in very anointed worship and praise. Suddenly out of "left field" this thought came to me: Hmmm! What if it isn't like this?

Jesus quickly countered: "What if it is? You mean the biggest event in all of history, the Wedding Feast of the Lamb, will take place and you're not going to have a rehearsal, you're not going to dream dreams about what it will be like?"

At that moment, the song from Jeremiah was being sung: "A song shall be heard in the cities of Judah. The voice of joy and the voice of gladness, the voice of the bridegroom and the voice of the bride."

I was quick to repent and forever remember a lesson I won't forget until He comes in glory!

We praise You, O God, as we want to praise, rejoice, be glad, and give You glory for all eternity. The wedding day of the Lamb hasn't come yet, but it is very near. We, Your bride, are getting ourselves ready for that biggest event in all of history. We thank You and praise You, O God, for inviting us, for calling us, for readying us for the Wedding Feast of the Lamb.

While we await that day let our songs be heard in the cities of Judah, in the streets of Jerusalem, and across the face of the earth. "The voice of joy and the voice of gladness, the voice of the bridegroom and the voice of the bride" (Jeremiah 33:11).

Maranatha! Come Lord Jesus! Come in glory!

53

EXALT YOUR GLORY

My heart is steadfast, O God, my heart is steadfast. I will sing and chant praise. Awake, O my soul; awake lyre and harp; I will wake the dawn. I will give thanks to you among the peoples, O Lord. I will chant your praise among the nations. For your kindness towers to the heavens, and your faithfulness to the skies. Be exalted above the heavens, O God, over all the earth be your glory.

(Ps 108:2-6) (NAB)

"For Thou, O Lord, art high above all the earth,
Thou art exalted far above all gods.
We exalt Thee, we exalt Thee,
We exalt Thee, O God."

PERHAPS NO OTHER SONG has the potential to bring worshippers into the realm of pure praise, worship, adoration, as Peter Sanchez's song, "We Exalt Thee."

To the degree that we exalt and lift up our God in daily worship, praise, and thanksgiving, to that degree we are graced to live our life task by task, hour by hour, day by day, in right order.

Keep my heart, O God, steadfast in praising You for Your great glory in the heavens and across the earth. "Be exalted O God above the heavens and let Your glory be over all the earth." Let this psalm song be on my heart this day. With every beat of my heart, I want to say: "I exalt You, O God, for You alone are high." Therefore I can be as lowly as they come. "For You alone are high."

"Over all the earth be your glory" (Ps 108). That includes the corners of the earth that have never heard Your Message, those who have heard a distorted message, and those who have heard the truth, accepted it, and now march to the beat of a "different drummer." May they all come to know You and Your glory in all of its fullness.

Keep our hearts steadfast in the Truth of who You are and the Truth of what we can do. We exalt Thee! We exalt Thee, O God!

I unite with all peoples across the face of the earth exalting Your glory this day in song and in prayer: We exalt Thee! We exalt Thee! We exalt Thee, O God!

54

MAJESTY OF GLORY YOUR WORK

I will give thanks to the Lord with all my heart in the company and the assembly of the just. Great are the works of the Lord, exquisite in all their delights. Majesty and glory are his work and his justice endures forever.

(Ps 111:1-6) (NAB)

WHAT A WORD for a world that is seeking justice. Majesty and glory are God's work and God's justice endures forever. Somehow in the midst of all the world's tragedies, I can praise You that Your justice endures forever.

Holy and awesome is Your name. You have not neglected Your people. Blessed be the name of the Lord now and forever.

From the rising to the setting of the sun is the name of the Lord to be praised. Praise the Lord today as the sun rises and again have some deliberate praise as it sets.

Join your praise with that of King David and his descendants in glory. Know that some day and then for all eternity I will give thanks to You together with all the blessed forever and ever.

Father God, I praise You for what I see and for what I fail to see. You know in whole that which I know only in part.

Your justice—not man's—endures forever. I praise You today for what I do not see in the justice systems of our world. Help me today to do at least one thing to bring about a more just and equitable world. In faith I believe Your Word: "Majesty and glory are Your work. Your justice endures forever!"

I may have to wait a few years to see it happen, but I have the assurance of Your Word that it will happen: "Your justice endures forever."

55

ABOVE THE HEAVENS YOUR GLORY

Yours, O Lord, are grandeur and power, majesty, splendor, and glory. For all in heaven and on earth is yours; yours, O Lord, is the sovereignty; you are exalted as head over all.

(1 Chr 29:11) (NAB)

"HIGH ABOVE ALL NATIONS is the Lord, above the heavens is his glory. Who is like the Lord our God who is enthroned on high?"

No one! No one! Absolutely no one!

Who is like our God?

No one who has ever lived to achieve fame for their riches, for their possessions, for their achievements, is like You. No one, absolutely no one, is like You, O Lord God! Not Moses, not an Alexander, a David, a Judith, an Esther, an Einstein, a Michaelangelo! No one, not an artist, an architect, an inventor, a designer, a writer, a statesman, a politician, a preacher of the Word!

No one, absolutely no one, is like You, O God. Yet You call us all by grace to become like to You and to share in Your glory. Is life worth living? Is it high adventure? Life with You is high adventure! Life with You is worth living!

"We were therefore buried with him through baptism into death in order that, just as Christ was raised from the dead through the glory of the Father, we too may live a new life" (Rom 6:4).

Your glory, O God, is above the heavens! We can sing it! We can shout it! We can quietly proclaim it in the citadel of our hearts.

"No one is like You, O God. From the rising to the setting of the sun, the name of the Lord is to be praised!" If there is

nothing else on our day's agenda, that would be enough to make our day full, our life worth living and our eternity assured.

Above the heavens is Your glory, O God! Today! Tomorrow! For all eternity!

56

TO YOUR NAME GLORY

Not to us, O Lord, not to us but to your name give glory because of your kindness, because of your truth. Our God is in heaven; whatever he wills he does. The house of Israel trusts in the Lord he is their help and their shield.

(Ps 115:1,3,9) (NAB)

A GLORY STORY comes to mind.

"To Your Name give glory!"

It began with my hearing that someone had said something "not nice" about my life.

I was furious. While in the act of graphically expressing my fury someone else said to me: "What difference will it make one hundred years from now?"

"But it's *my* life!" I was quick to retort.

"Whose?" I heard Jesus ask.

"Mine!" I swiftly retorted.

"Whose?" He questioned.

"Mine!" I meekly defended.

"Whose?" Jesus one more time questioned.

"Yours!" I finally yielded.

As I did I could sense Jesus winking at me. "Not to us but to Your name give glory."

Let us continue today to praise the Lord for His faithfulness even when we are not that faithful. Let us be quick to hear His voice and repent of all the subtle ways we take back our lives especially when we feel someone has wronged us and we need to be our own defense.

You are a faithful God! We continue to praise Your greatness and Your goodness in our lives. Through the power of Your Holy Name protect us from all who would slander our good

name. In the Name of Jesus, with the Blood of Jesus and with the Word of Jesus, we free those who would speak evil to think new thoughts and to feel new feelings.

Not to us but to Your name be glory, honor, and praise forever. For our families and nation we paraphrase Your psalm: The house of the U.S.A. trusts in God. You are our help and our shield. You remember us and bless us.

We bless the name of the Lord forever.

57

CLAIMING THE GLORY

I will give thanks to you, O Lord, with all my heart, [for you have heard the words of my mouth;] in the presence of the angels I will sing your praise; I will worship at your holy temple and give thanks to your name. Because of your kindness and your truth; for you have made great above all things your name and your promise. When I called you answered me; you built up strength within me. All the kings of the earth shall give thanks to you, O Lord, when they hear the words of your mouth. And they shall sing of the ways of the Lord: "Great is the glory of the Lord."

(Ps 138:1-5) (NAB)

TODAY LET US PRAY that all the leaders of the world may hear the words of Your mouth, O God. Let this be the platform on which they run for office, that they hear and they repeat the words of Your mouth.

"And they shall sing of the ways of the Lord:
'Great is the glory of the Lord'" (Ps 138:5).

Sometime ago I was giving a teaching in La Jolla, California on Spiritual Olympics and how to get rich for the Kingdom. I was exhorting my listeners to believe the amazing promises of Jesus to His disciples and to us:

"You will do all that I do and greater things!"

"You will preach the Gospel to the ends of the earth with signs and wonders following: the blind will see, the lame walk, the deaf hear, lepers be cleansed, the dead raised."

"You will cast out evil spirits. You will speak in new tongues. You will preach the Gospel to the ends of the earth."

As I was exhorting my listeners to believe all these astonishing promises of Jesus to us, His followers, the anointing for what I was declaring got stronger and stronger. Anything I had on my paper was no longer relevant. The words were flowing from me like a fountain. Finally this is what poured forth from my lips: "You need to remember *Who* it is *Who* is making all these promises. It is not a politician running for Office promising to reduce the National Debt. It is Jesus, the Eternal Son of the Father, saying: 'Read My Lips!'"

Yes, God, I desire to read Your lips, to remember Your promises for I know that they will all find fulfillment both in my lifetime and in eternity. Heaven and earth can pass away but not a word You have spoken nor a promise You have given will pass away without being fulfilled.

I pray a blessing today on our nation and its elected leaders. I pray that all our elected leaders may hear the words of Your mouth, and give thanks to You with all of their hearts. "For the glory of the Lord is great" (Ps 138:5). May they seek Your glory O Lord, and the good of Your people across the face of the earth.

58

TELL OF HIS GLORY

**Let all your works give you thanks, O Lord and let
your faithful ones bless you. Let them discourse of the
glory of your kingdom and speak of your might.**

(Ps 145:10-11) (NAB)

"WHAT DID WE EVER TALK ABOUT before we talked about Jesus?"
This was the remark of John, our driver, to Sister Ethel and me as
we were traveling from Minnesota to Colorado for a Full Gospel
Businessmen's Convention in the 1970s. John had totaled ten cars
before joining AA and then our Charismatic prayer group.

It was a nine-hour trip. A major part of our nine-hour conversation was about the glory of God's Kingdom and the power
of God's might. "Let them discourse of the glory of your kingdom
and speak of your might" (Ps 145:11) (NAB).

We never came to an ending where everything that could be
said was said, only new beginnings. It was like the conclusion of
John's Gospel where John the Apostle remarks: "There are still
many other things that Jesus did, yet if they were written about
in detail, I doubt there would be room enough in the entire world
to hold the books to record them" (Jn 21:25) (NAB).

*Let all your works give You thanks, O Lord, and let Your
faithful ones bless You! Even as they bless You, let them talk
about the glory of Your kingdom and speak of Your might!
Make known to all in our families, churches, and nations, the
glory of Your might and the glorious splendor of Your
kingdom. For Your kingdom is a kingdom for all ages and
Your dominion endures through all generations.*

*The Lord is faithful in all His words and holy in all His
works. Yes, Mighty God, You are faithful and holy in all Your
works. Let Your faithful ones bless You!*

59

GOD-SIZED GLORY

Praise the name of the Lord for his name alone is exalted. His majesty is above earth and heaven and he has lifted up the horn of his people. Be this his praise from all his faithful ones, from the children of Israel, his people close to him.

(Ps 148:13-14) (NAB)

HOW OFTEN HAVE I REJOICED in the beautiful relationship of Yahweh with His faithful servants: Abraham, Isaac, Jacob, Joseph, Moses, Joshua, Samuel, David, Judith, Esther, Deborah, Isaiah, Jeremiah, and Jonah. Relationships are a two-way street. The other side of the coin is the beautiful relationship Yahweh's faithful servants had with Yahweh.

We are living in the age of the experience of God. All of us have a God-sized vacuum that cannot be filled with anything but a deeper and deeper experience of the living God. No matter what we have going for our lives, if we do not have an experience of the living God to go with it, it is like ashes in the mouth.

We could have money so vast we could never spend it. We could have power and prestige the world would envy. We could have education beyond our intelligence but if we do not have an experience of the living God to go with it—it is all like ashes in the mouth.

I choose intimacy with You, O God, beyond every other good in life. Draw me into an ever deeper and deeper experience of Your love. I rejoice today for the beautiful relationship Your faithful servants had with You. Help me by Your Spirit to rejoice in and to imitate the faith and trust of Abraham, the intimacy of Moses, the courage of Judith, the valor of Deborah, and the steadfastness of Job. Help me to keep my heart, my mind, and my spirit open and expectant for an ever-deepening experience of You, the Living God.

60

GLORY OF ALL THE FAITHFUL

Sing to the Lord a new song of praise in the assembly
of the faithful. Let Israel be glad in their maker, let
the children of Zion rejoice in their king. Let them
praise his name in the festive dance, let them sing
praise to him with timbrel and harp. For the Lord
loves his people and he adorns the lowly with victory.
Let the faithful exult in glory, let them sing for joy
upon their couches, let the high praises of God be in
their throats. This is the glory of all his faithful.

(Ps 149:1-6,9) (NAB)

THE "HIGH PRAISES" OF GOD is the glory of the church, the glory of
all the faithful, all nations, and all denominations.

In almost thirty years of attending conferences in the
Charismatic Renewal, I have never heard the high praises of God
like I did in the Cathedral Church of Dominica, West Indies in
May of 1996.

"Hands and Heart to Build the Church" was the theme of
their conference. A word that God gave me to declare was: If you
want to see the miracle power of God, declare God's Presence to
meet their need.

Many of the 2,500 in attendance had never prayed in
tongues. A new prayer language "to build the Church" was a
need. The Lord's direction was simply to declare His presence to
meet their need for empowerment, for healing, for deliverance,
for signs and for wonders!

My directions were simple: "Turn your eyes on Jesus your
Baptizer in the Holy Spirit. Ask Jesus to release that new praise
language within you. Humming is the same in every language.
Begin humming. Neutral syllables are the same in every language. Let yourself hear the sounds." Instantly a crescendo of
humming and neutral sounds filled the Cathedral.

Under an anointing more powerful than any I had ever experienced, I declared God's word: "Open your mouth and I will fill it!" Twenty-five hundred mouths shot open like hungry birds on a spring day and God filled them with "high praises!"

The explosion of sound all but swept Monsignor John Lewis off his feet as he carried the Blessed Sacrament into the Cathedral. High praises of God flooded the place. As each need arose, God empowered us to carefully and caringly set free all those in need of deliverance.

Witness time confirmed that just as Jesus did throughout Scripture, He went through the Cathedral and healed everyone. The crippled walked, the deaf heard, the blind could see, cancer and arthritis were cured in that holy place.

Reports of the conference went far and wide. The evening news reported: When Father Elveau told his parishioners what happened at the Cathedral, the church shook as though by an earthquake.

O Lord God, we, too, say "Yes" to being shaken out of our complacency into the full experience of all Your gifts. Your power and Your glory. Release in us not just the gift of tongues but the "high praises" Your Holy Word speaks about. "This is the glory of all the faithful." This is something we will be doing for all eternity and so we would like to begin as the Dominicans did! Right now!

61

SOVEREIGN MAJESTY
AND GLORY

"Praise the Lord in his sanctuary, praise him in the
firmament of his strength. Praise him for his mighty
deeds, praise him for his sovereign majesty. Praise
him with the blast of the trumpet, praise him with
lyre and harp. Praise him with timbrel and dance,
praise him with strings and pipe. Praise him with
sounding cymbals, praise him with clanging cymbals.
Let everything that has breath praise the Lord!
Alleluia.

(Ps 150:1-6) (NAB)

TODAY IN A FINAL DOXOLOGY with full orchestra, with all the stops
of our heart pulled out, let us praise the Lord of the universe "for
His sovereign majesty."

Sovereign majesty means that His majesty has supreme
power. There is no power above Him. There is no power that is
not below Him. He is over all, above all, reigning as Lord of the
universe.

Why then do we not bring to His sovereign majesty all the
needs, all the challenges, all the poverty that plagues the world
we live in. Either we really believe in the world of the supernatural or we do not. If we truly believe, then it needs to be
shown in what we think, say, and do.

"Pray for a sovereign move of My Spirit," the Lord once said
to me.

I asked, "What do you mean sovereign?"

"Sovereign move means My power to match Your need."

I have discovered over the years that when you pray for a
sovereign move, that is what you get. A sovereign move of the
power of God to match your need, whatever that need is.

Many times in my Kamehameha Prayer Pantry, I felt God's
power to meet my need. I felt I had within me a full orchestra to

strike up His praises when I desired to flood this place with His praises. I felt I had a whole army of intercessors when I needed to intercede for myself, my writing, my family, my religious Order, my church, my nation, the nations of the world.

Loving God, none of us can really add anything to Your greatness by our praise of You. Yet You desire a full orchestra of praise from each of our hearts that we in turn might be blessed, empowered, strengthened, made whole and holy. Do a mighty work in us and we will continue to praise and bless Your name forever and ever!

Let there be a sovereign move of Your Holy Spirit in each of our lives today and in the lives of all we love or are called to intercede for. Let Your power match our need!

62

GRACE AND GLORY

I had rather one day in your courts than a thousand elsewhere; I had rather lie at the threshold of the house of my God than dwell in the tents of the wicked. For a sun and a shield is the Lord God to me grace and glory he bestows; the Lord withholds no good thing from those who walk in sincerity.

(Ps 84:11-12) (NAB)

I HAD RATHER ONE DAY HERE in my Kamehameha Prayer Pantry than a thousand elsewhere on the most sought after islands on the face on the earth.

I had rather one day here on the threshold of the house of my God than to dwell in the tents of the wicked. One day at God's doorstep than a thousand on the world's thrones.

"For a sun and a shield is the Lord God to me" (Ps 84:12). We are a culture both searching for more and more sun and paying more and more for shields from the sun.

How great to be able to pray: "You alone are my sun and my shield; grace and glory You bestow." There is no second guessing this. It is the truth: If I am to have my daily fill of grace and glory then I need to claim the word from Psalm 84.

God withholds no good thing from those who walk in sincerity. Today's grace is to walk in sincerity and truth. The truth of Who God is and the truth of who I am.

"Enter into My presence
 that you may know me as the Great I Am,
 the Absolute, the Irresistible, the Infinite,
 the Omnipresent, the Omniscient, the Omnipotent,
 the King of kings, the Lord of lords.
When you truly come to know the Great I Am, you
 will come to know the great you are."

The Lord recently added this one-liner for me: "When you come to know *who* you are, then you will know *what* you can do."

O Lord God, help me to spend this one day in Your courts delighting in the grace and glory You bestow. You are the source of all good things for me. You are my shield, my protection, from all that could harm or destroy. I claim and proclaim that I had rather this one day in Your courts than a thousand elsewhere.

O God, keep me in Your presence this day. Where else can I find my delight? Where else can I come to know You as You are known? Where else can I come to truly know who I am and what it is that You call me to do?

63

GLORY OF HIS FAVOR

Yet the Lord is waiting to show you favor, and he rises to pity you: For the Lord is God of justice; blessed are all who wait for him! . . . He will be gracious to you when you cry out, as soon as he hears he will answer you. . . . No longer will your Teacher hide himself, but with your own eyes you shall see your Teacher. 'This is the way; walk in it.'

(Is 30:18-21) (NAB)

HOW OFTEN HAVE WE BEEN confronted with the need to make a decision only to respond: "I'll pray about it." And so we do. "Lord, what would You have me to do?" is a prayer often on the lips of Christians.

I recall one time I got involved in something questionable. Before I began the writing of *We, the Bride,* I asked a small group with strong gifts of discernment to ask the Lord if there was anything in me that could block the full power of the Spirit for my writing.

Father Carl had this initial discernment: "I don't know if you'll like this, but God is saying, 'For you it is the Enneagram.'"

"The Enneagram! Nothing wrong with that!" I was quick to defend it.

Several years before as a community we had studied the Enneagram. It was fascinating enough for each of us to buy our own book in order to learn how we relate to one another according to the number we are on the Enneagram.

Looking back on my journey with the "E", I realize there was never any discerning about it, but more like a secret pride that we were both knowledgeable and able to discuss the "in" thing.

"Tell me what's wrong with the Enneagram?" I pressed Father Carl, my discerner, for an answer.

"Go ask God!"

I did and heard, "So you really want to know!"

"Yes, I want to know."

"For you it is subtly shifting your life—from under My Lordship—and helping you to be lord one more time."

Then God showed me how in the middle of a very anointed talk I could be heard saying, "What else can you expect from a Number 7 on the Enneagram?" As I did this I was placing my life and declaring my identity—more under who I was on the Enneagram—than who I was under the Lordship of Jesus Christ. For me it was a very subtle way to snatch back my life, to get back some of the controls to bring about my own wholeness and holiness. What I didn't know was that, rather than creating light and freedom, it was generating darkness and bondage in me.

"God, I get the point. But how come I got hooked on the Enneagram?"

"You never asked Me!" (True, it was as simple as that. I never once prayed to discern if this was something God wanted me to study. I just did it.)

"God, I repent. Cleanse my mind, my heart, my spirit with your Precious Blood so I may hear Your voice for my writing."

God is faithful. He set me free to "let go and to let God."

This has been my experience. I am grateful for it. I pray that God may use it to help others sort out what is life-giving for their life. Life is short! If we use our energies on something less than His will, we do not have the energy we need for doing His perfect will.

Jesus, You are the Way, the Truth, and the Life. Thank You for showing me the way, revealing for me the truth, and calling me more and more to let go of all I do not need to live out Your life in me.

64

GLORY, HONOR AND POWER

You are worthy, O Lord our God, to receive glory and honor and power, for you created all things, and by your will they were created and have their being.

(Rv 4:11)

TODAY LET US GIVE THAT GLORY, honor and power to our Lord and God. He is worthy to receive far beyond any measure than we could give in time and in eternity. You, Lord God, have created all things. All that we see, all that is beyond our seeing. By Your will there are trillions of stars in the sky, countless grains of sand on the seashore, gigantic glaciers of snow and ice, magnificent mountainsides of tropical growth, acres of waving grain, immense oceans of teeming life, profuse forests with countless game and wildlife, glorious flowers of infinite variety and hue.

All have been called to give You glory by their existence!

I give You the glory, honor and praise for all You have created from the beginning of time till now and all that ever will be. You are worthy to receive glory and honor and power, for You created all things and by Your will they came to be. Today I desire to give You the glory, honor and praise for all that You have created especially for what is in my front yard, in my back yard and on my deck.

I can never thank You enough for all that is glory and beauty in my life and in the lives of those I love. True, I can never thank You enough, but let today go on record as a day when I really tried fittingly to thank You!

65

FILLED WITH HIS GLORY

Praise be to his glorious name forever; may the whole earth be filled with his glory. Amen and Amen.

(Ps 72:19) (NAB)

"To be where you are powerfully used is not where it is at, but to be where you are totally surrendered." God gave this word to me sometime ago. Now it came back with a whole new significance. "To be where I am totally surrendered."

As my days in Hawaii went by, I did everything I could to give God a blank check saying: "Show me what to do and I will do it. Call me to repentance and I will repent. Open the door and I will walk through it. Give me a prayer and I will pray it. Put on my heart a new song and I will sing it. I have come to do Your will, O God."

From the rising to the setting of the sun, I was in a place to live in God's Presence. All around me was such beauty, peace and glory. All around me the reflection of a God who is total beauty, peace and glory!

"Allow Me to love you in a thousand ways every day." That word came back with a whole new significance and impact. "Allow Me to love you. Only as you feel loved, will you be able to believe what I am ready to do."

One day as I was about to snap a gorgeous picture, of an ethereal sky bottomed by glimmering iridescent waters, and flanked by a dark foliated shoreline, I heard: "That's a 'God-mark' card. It says 'With love from your Father.'"

O God, the world is full of "God-mark" cards scrawled "With love from your Father." How can I ever thank You. All is gift.

"Let them give glory to the Lord and proclaim His praise in the islands." With all my heart, all my soul, all my mind and strength, I desire to give You the glory and the praise due to Your name. This is a time of my life when I want to be lavish in my praise of Your glory, Your goodness, Your love. "Praise be to your glorious name forever; may the whole earth be filled with your glory. Amen and Amen" (Ps 72:19).

66

GLORY OF HIS HERITAGE

Therefore, I, too, hearing of your faith in the Lord Jesus and of your love for all the holy ones, do not cease giving thanks for you, remembering you in my prayers, that the God of our Lord Jesus Christ, the Father of glory, may give you a spirit of wisdom and revelation resulting in knowledge of him. May the eyes of your hearts be enlightened, that you may know what is the hope that belongs to his call, what are the riches of glory in his inheritance among the holy ones, and what is the surpassing greatness of his power for us who believe in accord with the exercise of his great might, which he worked in Christ, raising him from the dead and seating him at his right hand in the heavens.

(Eph 1:15-20) (NAB)

"YOU HAVE GIVEN ME your heart. Now give Me your mind." It was the early days of the renewal. I was not used to God asking big things of me so I was quick to object. "Wait a minute, God. That's all I have left."

The call was persistent so I asked for the grace to do just that. I have learned to pray a lot to Jesus, Incarnate Wisdom, for the gift of wisdom. Wisdom is a gift to know what to do with all the other gifts.

Both wisdom and revelation are ongoing mind gifts. We grow in them as we use them for God's glory. Paul prayed for these gifts for his converts. "Each of us has received God's favor in the measure in which Christ bestows it. Thus you find Scripture saying: 'When he ascended on high, he took a host of captives and gave gifts to all'" (Eph 4:7) (NAB).

God, I want to love You today with my whole heart, my whole soul and my whole mind. In ways fitting with the riches of Your wisdom and revelation, I yield my mind to Your working. Come with "Your giant bulldozer," the Holy Spirit, and do a massive work of clearing away all the rubbish and all that is no longer useful or helpful for the work that You would do in and through my mind.

Grant to me in ever greater measure the gifts of wisdom and revelation as "Godspell" phrases it: "That I may know You more clearly, love You more dearly and follow You more nearly."

67

FUN IN GLORY

When the Lord brought back the captives of Zion, we were like men dreaming. Then our mouth was filled with laughter, and our tongue with rejoicing.

(Ps 126:1-2) (NAB)

"YOU ARE MY FUN BRIDE," Jesus said to me one day.

"Why do You call me Your fun bride?" I questioned.

"Because you are fun! You do the most unusual things in your prayer times like the day you decided to toast Me and I toasted you back."

One night on the North Shore, looking up at my picture of Jesus coming again in glory, I toasted: "To Jesus, my Bridegroom, who is coming soon." Jesus toasted back: "To Frannie, My bride, who can hardly wait until I come."

"To Jesus, my Bridegroom, who is full of surprises!" "To Frannie, My bride, who is also full of surprises."

"To Jesus, who can tell it like it is, and keep me in my place, when I feel inclined to be all over the place." "To Frannie, My bride, who is willing to hear it like it is!"

"To Jesus, my Bridegroom, who holds His arms out in constant welcome to me, that I can know the love of a Bridegroom for a bride." "To Frannie, My bride, who is ready, willing, and eager to receive the love that I have had for her for all eternity."

"To Jesus, my Bridegroom, who has supplied and is able to supply all my needs, even supplying some of my wants." "To Frannie, My Bride, who is willing to own the difference between needs and wants."

"To Jesus, my Bridegroom, who has called me to stillness, to listen for the still small voice that can only be heard in silence." "To Frannie, My Bride, who said it's okay what I don't hear, what I don't see, that I am just called to believe."

"To Jesus, my Bridegroom, who has led me from Genesis to Malachi through stories of glory." "To Frannie, My bride, who has not only found delight but tears as she followed through the stories of Yahweh's faithfulness and the Chosen People's unfaithfulness."

"To Jesus, my Bridegroom, who stood with me as I wept tears for the joy in the heart of the Father when I realized You and Your Mother were the only ones born of woman who never fell short of the glory." "To Frannie, My bride, for each tear you shed was a joy to My heart, like a precious jewel, a gem for your crown."

Yahweh, truly we ought to weep when we realize that everyone who ever lived, even Moses, Your intimate friend, fell short of the glory. We ought to weep, Jesus, when we realize what an incredible joy You are to Your Father's heart. Through the infinite power of Your death and Resurrection, may we be enabled more and more like Peter to weep for our sins and to live in victory until You come in glory. Come Lord Jesus! Come quickly! Come in glory!

68

GAZING ON THE GLORY

Hear, O son, O daughter, and see; turn your ear, forget
your people and your father's house. So shall the
King desire your beauty; for he is your Lord, and you
must worship him. All glorious are the King's
daughters and sons as they enter; their raiment is
threaded with spun gold. In embroidered apparel
they are borne in to the King; behind them the virgins
of their train are brought to you.

(Ps 45:11-15) (NAB)

As THE SPIRIT WOULD LEAD I often came back to that whimsical
way to pray: To toast our soon coming Bridegroom and King. It
freed me to know that the world of the supernatural is more real
than the material world we live in. The Throne of my Bridegroom
King is more real than the chair that I am sitting on.

More than that—it is more lasting. "All things are passing.
All will disappear 'like the flowers of the field'" (Jas 1:10).

"But the word of the Lord endures forever" (1 Pt 1:25).

"All of us, gazing on the Lord's glory with unveiled faces,
are being transformed from glory to glory into his very image by
the Lord who is the Spirit" (2 Cor 3:18) (NAB). Folks, it is happening. There is no stopping this miraculous, sovereign moving
of the Holy Spirit across the face of the earth.

More today than yesterday. More tomorrow than last week.
It is happening. We are being transformed, our family, our
church, our nation, the nations of the world are being transformed, from grace to grace, light to light, glory to glory into His
very image by the Lord who is the Spirit. This is not something
we are programming in our church or home computers. But it is
programmed into God's computer. It is moving toward fulfillment. Only God can teach us what that means and so we pray:

What bliss, Lord Jesus, in our faith imagination to gaze upon Your glory with unveiled faces. As we do we are being transformed from our unbelief to belief, from our lack of trust to trust, from our lack of love to love You with our whole heart, soul and strength. We "are being transformed from glory to glory into Your very image by the Lord who is the Spirit." None of us will ever be the same again after this prayer time today. Our King desires our beauty for He is Lord and we must worship Him.

69

YOUR GLORY ONLY

Let them praise the name of the Lord, for his name alone is exalted; His splendor is above the earth and the heavens.

(Ps 148:13) (NRS)

IT IS IN THE MIND as well as the heart that our battles are lost or won. Sometime ago the Lord gave to me this prophetic promise which has helped me a lot:

I gift you with the power to be single-minded before Me
with My mind.
It is true that My thoughts are above your thoughts like the
heavens are above the earth,
but more and more you will discover
that My thoughts are indeed your thoughts.
I am as close to you as your next thought.
Yield your mind to My mind, and I will gift you with
discernment to quickly see the thoughts
that come from the Holy Spirit, your human spirit or
the evil spirit.
I will give you the power to switch from what is useless or
evil as easily as you switch TV Channels.

Father, I ask for the grace to be single-minded before You with Your mind. I believe that You are as close to me as my next thought. Forgive me for all the ways I have used my mind that have not been for Your glory and Your praise. You know the times I have wasted watching a TV show that Your Spirit clearly showed me was neither from You nor for me.

Forgive me this wrong-doing. Truly in allowing this I have fallen short of the glory for which You created me. Grant to me an ever greater gift of discernment and the grace to use it wisely for the coming of Your Kingdom.

To discern what is from the Kingdom of Light and what is from the Kingdom of Darkness is perhaps one of the greatest needs among God's people today. Pour out this gift in miraculous measure on Your church, on Your people, and on my life! Thank You, God!

70

PLANS FOR YOUR GLORY

The Lord answer you in time of distress; the name of the God of Jacob defend you! May he send you help from the sanctuary, from Zion may he sustain you. May he grant you what is in your heart and fulfill your every plan. May we shout for joy at your victory and raise the standards in the name of our God. The Lord grant all your requests!

(Ps 20:2-6) (NAB)

WHAT IS IN YOUR HEART TODAY? What are the desires of your heart for yourself, for a loved one? May God grant you the desires of your heart and fulfill your every plan.

What are your desires? What are your plans? Can you make a list today and say "God, I trust You to give me the desires of my heart and to fulfill my every plan?"

Sometimes our dilemma or puzzlement is that we just don't know the desires of our hearts or we are fearful that our desires might be different from God's desires for us. In times like these a good prayer to pray is: "Lord increase in me the desire for what You want and decrease anything that You don't want for me."

God, I trust You with the desires of my heart. I trust You to fulfill my every plan. Right now I turn over every plan of mine to Your divine scrutiny that You may show me where my thoughts are not Your thoughts nor my plans Your plans. One by one, let us talk about them today. One by one, show me what is only mine and what is truly Your plan for my life.

You see my heart. Whatever is not of You, take it so I may truly trust that You can grant me "whatever is in my heart and fulfill my every plan."

71

THE POWER AND THE GLORY

Shout for joy, O daughter Zion! Sing joyfully, O Israel! Be glad and exult with all your heart, O daughter Jerusalem! The Lord has removed the judgment against you, He has turned away your enemies; the King of Israel, the Lord, is in your midst, you have no further misfortune to fear. On that day, it shall be said to Jerusalem: Fear not, O Zion, be not discouraged! The Lord, your God, is in your midst, a mighty savior; He will rejoice over you with gladness, and renew you in his love, He will sing joyfully because of you, as one sings at festivals.

(Zep 3:14-18) (NAB)

THIS IS THE DAY when the Father will dance as He rejoices over you with gladness. He renews you in His love. He sings joyfully because of you. Rejoice for what you have in Jesus. Together you stand in veiled but real victory before your Father. You are two in one—Bridegroom and bride in the heart of your Father.

Two in one in the Heart of the Father. What a place to be! What a reality to know!

I am reminded of a happening some years ago when Sister Lucienne and I were asked to pray for a very troubled woman who had been delivered from many spirits. She knew that three demonic strongholds still held her in their grip. One was the spirit of automatic handwriting.

I really did not want to be part of the group praying. But when we asked the Lord, He said, "Yes, you are to pray for her."

A small group of intercessors began praising God for what He would do. Instantly the woman's hands gnarled up grotesquely and the demon cried out: "You can't cast me out! You're not fasting."

Fright hit me. In the same instant, a greater reality revived me.

Under the anointing, I countered the word of the demon that spoke: "I am a Bride of Jesus Christ, the King of kings and the Lord of lords. He fasted for forty days and forty nights for me in the desert. We are two in one in the Heart of the Father. I claim the power of His fasting in my body. In His name, by His authority, and with His power, I bind your power and cast you out."

Instantly the demonic power was gone. The deliverance was complete! The woman was totally free. The hands that had been used by the enemy for automatic handwriting were lifted up in praise of Jesus.

"When you know who you are, then you will know what you can do," Jesus assures us.

Jesus, we are no match for the power of the Powers of Darkness. But You are! Help us on our journey to keep believing You for the incredible and the impossible! You promised us that these signs will follow those who believe (Mk 17). In Your Name, we will cast out evil. We believe that. Teach us by Your wisdom to exercise that power.

As we see the Powers of Darkness subject to You, let us remember Your words to the Apostles: "Rejoice not that demons are subject to you but that your names are written in heaven" (Lk 10:20).

72

PRISONERS OF GLORY

The nations will revere your name, Lord, and all the earthly kings your glory. When the Lord builds Zion again and shows himself in his glory, when he turns to hear the prayer of the destitute and does not spurn their prayer. This will be written down for future generations that people yet unborn may praise the Lord. The Lord looks down from his sanctuary on high from heaven he surveys the earth to hear the groaning of the prisoners and set free those under the sentence of death.

(Ps 102:15-20) (REB)

WHAT A PICTURE for today the Lord of glory looking down from the holy heights to hear the groans of prisoners and showing Himself in His glory to them! The psalmist says He turns to the prayer of the destitute and does not spurn their prayer.

Three thousand years ago, King David said: "Let this be recorded for future generations. Let this be written "the Lord desires to 'set free those under sentence of death.'"

The world knows the story of Jeffrey Dahmer's sentence to life in prison. What the world does not know is the rest of the story.

A friend of mine, Sister Giselda, O.S.F., has had a prison ministry for more than twenty years. When she visited Jeffrey's jail cell, he asked: "Is there any hope for me?" After some sharing of Jesus' love for even the most hardened sinners and the Scriptures to support it, Sister prayed the sinner's prayer with Jeffrey, and he accepted Jesus as his personal Savior.

Some time later when Jeffrey was saying good-bye as he was leaving for his "life-in-prison" sentence he remarked to Sister Giselda: "I know it's a life sentence, but it's not eternal life. I have been promised that by my God. I'll see you there."

One of my most precious years in ministry was the year I spent serving prisoners in a Federal Corrections Institute in Milan, Michigan. Some six hundred men were incarcerated there for everything from murder to stealing heroin the size of a tea bag from Vietnam. As Sister Lucienne and I prayed about responding to the invitation to minister there, God spoke these words: "Your only problem will be to believe what I am ready to do or to get in My way by claiming any of the glory."

I will never forget the day we prayed for Dave, a man so filled with hate that every time he got out of prison he was right back in. Dave had an ulcer so bad that he drank a whole bottle of Maalox every day just to tolerate bland foods.

His medical records showed recent transfusions of seventeen pints of blood. The doctor's report that morning was, "I'm sorry, Dave, but your stomach is one ulcerated mess and there is nothing more that doctors or medicine can do. You'll just have to live with it."

"God, You are bigger than any hate," we prayed, "and bigger than any ulcer. Heal Dave now. Thank You for doing it."

When we came back the next week Dave stood at the gate glowing. "I just gotta thank God and all you guys for what He did for me this last week. God really heard your prayers! I haven't got an ounce of hate left in me. The prison walls have disappeared. I know that they are there physically, but they are not there for me for I'm free inside.

"And that ulcer! Man, there's not a trace left of it! Sunday morning I had sausage and bacon for breakfast and pizza for lunch! What is even greater, I have begun praising God and I can't stop!"

"This will be written down for future generations that people yet unborn may praise the Lord" (Ps 102:18) (REB).

Here we are the future generation King David spoke of, praising the Lord three thousand years later for all those who have "fallen short of the glory" over the centuries, but have come to a saving knowledge of Jesus Christ as Lord, Savior, Healer.

Jesus, You are the Man for all Seasons for all of our lives! If we want to live in the liberty of the children of God and as heirs and heiresses of heaven, we need You! We thank You today for making possible the release of the captives according to Your law and for Your eternal glory. Bless all women and men who are serving out sentences of justice. Bless our justice system and ministers of justice. Have mercy on us all.

73

GOD OF GLORY WITHIN US

Now this is eternal life that they should know you, the one true God, and the one whom you sent, Jesus Christ. I glorified you on earth by accomplishing the work you gave me to do. Now glorify me Father, with you, with the glory that I had with you before the world began.

(Jn 17:3-5) (NAB)

MOTHER TERESA'S FAVORITE BOOK, *One With Jesus* by Paul deJaeger, is on the Indwelling Presence. Among other truths, Paul states: The greatest truth neglected in our Christian experience is the Indwelling Presence, the God of Glory living within us.

Reversely, the greatest truth for Christians to discover is that the Indwelling Presence, the God of glory, Father, Son, and Holy Spirit truly lives within us. When I neglect this awareness for even so short a time as several hours, I have found this confession life-giving: O God, I am sorry, that the past few hours I have been living my life independent of Yours. I have been living as though You, the God of glory, were not in the very center of my being, empowering my thoughts, my words, my actions. Forgive me for not being aware of Your presence. Forgive me for living my life independent of Your life.

Mother Teresa asked this question at the end of each day: "Lord, what did we do today together and what did I do alone?"

At the end of each day, I, too, need to ask: "Lord, what did we do together today and what did I do alone?" More than anything else I desire to be aware of Your presence within me ready to be part of every part of my life. Grant to me the grace of being more and more aware of Your Indwelling Presence. Jesus, You have given me the glory that the Father gave to You that I also may be one with my brothers and sisters as You are one with the Father.

74

"DELIGHT IN THE LORD" GLORY

Trust in the Lord and do good, so you will live in the land and enjoy security. Take delight in the Lord, and he will give you the desires of your heart. Commit your way to the Lord, trust in him, and he will act.

(Ps 37:3-5) (NRS)

DISCERNMENT IS PERHAPS one of the most needed and most neglected of the gifts of the Spirit. The New Testament is clear about the need for "discernment of spirits." John says clearly, "Test the spirits." How we do this has been expounded on and written in detail by spiritual writers through the ages.

One of the simplest 1-2-3 approaches, that has proven effective for me and for others in living out a genuine Christian life, is to ask for discernment of the Holy Spirit from your Baptism and Confirmation to be activated in you. To know what to do in a particular situation can be as simple as:

1. Your heart says it.
2. Scripture confirms it.
3. The circumstances are right.

Often people have expressed to me their desire to some day go on a Pilgrimage to Israel. It has been the desire of their heart for a long time. I ask them if they have ever claimed it as God's promise to them in the Word. In Psalm 37 it says: "Take delight in the Lord, and he will grant you your heart's requests." Find Psalm 37 and write in the margin: Holy Land . . . Jerusalem.

Lord God, in You is all truth, all light, all wisdom, all knowledge. Give to me a quickness of Spirit to check with You the paths You want me to follow. Let me know what leads to Your greater glory and what I can well do without.

Pour out today a new measure of Your gift of discernment

into my life. Show me the desires of Your heart and grant to me the desires of my heart.

I give You permission to meet me where I am at. I desire that the desires of Your heart become the desires of my heart. Confirm what You are calling me to with a word from Your Word. Speak through my circumstances that I may clearly know Your will for my life.

75

GLORY OF INTERCESSION

Therefore, he is always able to save those who approach God through him, since he lives forever to make intercession for them.

(Heb 7:25) (NAB)

In the same way, the Spirit too comes to the aid of our weakness. For we do not know how to pray as we ought, but the Spirit itself intercedes with inexpressible groanings. And the one who searches hearts knows what is the intention of the Spirit, because it intercedes for the holy ones according to God's will.

(Rom 8:26-27) (NAB)

AT THE FOOT OF THE CROSS, I let go of my sinfulness. I let go of all the ways that I have fallen short of the glory of God. In my Prayer Pantry, I had owned my sinfulness in thought, word, and deed. Memory by memory, picture by picture, reality by reality, commandment by commandment in those special oceanfront prayer times, I owned and then disowned all the Spirit showed me so that I might be clothed with the righteousness of Jesus.

Not only had I owned them for myself but in magnificent moments of intercession for others I could plead the righteousness of Jesus for all I was given to pray for.

In my prayer the Lord spoke: "You seek a plan for intercession. Look to Jesus for His plan. Stand clothed in His righteousness, agree with Jesus for the Father's perfect plan for those for whom you pray. Confess their sinfulness as your own. Come against all that opposes My plan. Bring down the enemy's strongholds in the minds of those for whom you pray. Claim their minds to be captive and obedient to the Lord Jesus Christ."

Intercessors are found all over the world. Intercession is rooted in the Old Testament, in Abraham, Moses, Joshua,

Jeremiah, Isaiah. Jesus is our greatest example of an intercessor. He spent thirty years in His Hidden Life, three years in ministry, and two thousand years in intercession.

The Catechism of the Catholic Church says: Intercession is a prayer of petition which leads us to pray as Jesus did. He is the one intercessor with the Father on behalf of all people, especially sinners. (Rom 8:34; 1 Jn 2:1; 1 Tim 2:5-8). He is "able for all time to save those who draw near to God through him, since he always lives to make intercession for them" (Heb 7:25).

"The Holy Spirit himself intercedes for us and intercedes for the saints according to the will of God" (Rom 8:26-27). Since Abraham, intercession—asking on behalf of another—has been characteristic of a heart attuned to God's mercy and God's glory.

Father, Son, and Holy Spirit, thank You for this plan of intercession. This has to be one of Your best and most needed gifts. Jesus, this is something that You have been doing for almost two thousand years—living to make intercession for us. I pray today for a double portion of this gift for myself and for the Church that none may be lost and all may be brought in Your time into the fullness of Your life in Your Kingdom.

76

AWAKENING TO GLORY

Lift up your heads, oh you gates; be lifted up, you ancient doors, that the King of glory may come in. Who is this King of glory? The Lord almighty, he is the King of glory.

(Ps 24:9-10)

Be exalted, O God, above the heavens; let your glory be over all the earth!

(Ps 57:11)

You shall see in your spirit this day a new awakening
    that will bring you into a new vision of the
    Majesty of your God,
        a vision not only of My tenderness,
        My love, and My mercy but also of My
        justice, My holiness, and My wrath.
As I did for Peter and Isaiah, I give you a vision of the
    sinfulness of sin and the holiness of your God.
As I do I call you to a constant and deeper repentance
    and a constant and deeper joy in your salvation.
We are living in the Age of Mercy. God doesn't expect
    us to be *perfect now.*
Sin is to say No when God is saying Yes...
    No to His love, His desire for intimacy,
        no to a revelation of His Glory.
    No to His Lordship over your life,
        no to a perpetuating Pentecost,
        no to a relationship to the Holy Spirit.
    No to a revelation of who Jesus is as Bridegroom.
        No to who you are as Bride...
Sin is to fall short of the Glory in thought, word,
    and deed.

Father, Son, and Holy Spirit, this day I ask Your Divine Mercy on my entire life. Forgive me for all the times that I have said No when You have said Yes. Forgive my skid marks all over the King's Highway. Empower me today to flow with Your plan for my life that all the days and ways of my life may give You glory.

77

FULL OF HIS GLORY

The mountains melt like wax before the Lord, before the God of all the earth. The heavens proclaim his righteousness, and all the nations behold his glory.

(Ps 97:5-6) (NRS)

GOD HAS GIVEN US a new day. Let us celebrate the fullness of His glory. Let us celebrate the glory of the Lord as David did in the Psalms:

"O Lord, our Lord, how majestic is your name in all the earth! You have set your glory above the heavens" (Ps 8:1).

"Lift up your heads, O you gates; be lifted up, you ancient doors, that the King of glory may come in" (Ps 24:7).

"Who is this King of glory? The Lord strong and mighty, the Lord mighty in battle" (Ps 24:8).

"I love the house where you live, O Lord, the place where your glory dwells" (Ps 26:8).

"Be exalted, O God, above the heavens; let your glory be over all the earth" (Ps 57:5).

"I have seen you in the sanctuary and beheld your power and your glory" (Ps 63:2).

"The heavens proclaim his righteousness, and all the peoples see his glory" (Ps 97:6).

"Praise be to your glorious name forever; may the whole earth be filled with your glory. Amen and Amen" (Ps 72:19).

David reassures us in Psalm 102:16, "For the Lord will rebuild Zion and appear in His glory."

"The whole earth is full of Your glory." This is the song on my heart today. That means continents, countries, states, churches, homes, hearts—yours, mine, family, friends, neighbors, are full of God's Glory.

The works of darkness may be increasing across the face of the earth but nothing compared with the works of light! The whole earth is full of Your glory, O God. That means North America, South America, Europe, Asia, Africa, Australia, the WHOLE EARTH is full of Your glory!

As King David did in the Psalms, I want to praise You as a God of glory and strength! You are a God of victory and triumph! I declare Your glory among all the nations of the earth. Be exalted above the heavens and let Your full glory be over all the earth. Forever and ever! Amen.

78

YOUR GOD, YOUR GLORY

The desert will burst into bloom, it will rejoice greatly and shout for joy. The glory of Lebanon will be given to it, the splendor of Carmel and Sharon; they will see the glory of the Lord, the splendor of our God.

(Is 35:2)

ALL OF THE GREAT PROPHETS experienced and spoke of the Glory of God. Perhaps Isaiah spoke of it more than any other.

"And the glory of the Lord will be revealed, and all mankind together will see it. For the mouth of the Lord has spoken" (Is 40:5).

"Then your light will break forth like the dawn, and your healing will quickly appear; then your righteousness (or your righteous one) will go before you, and the glory of the Lord will be your rear guard" (Is 58:8).

"See, darkness covers the earth and thick darkness is over the peoples, but the Lord rises upon you and his glory appears over you" (Is 60:2).

"The sun will no more be your light by day, nor will the brightness of the moon shine on you for the Lord will be your everlasting light, and your God will be your glory" (Is 60:19).

"Arise, shine, for your light has come,
     and the glory of the Lord rises upon you.
See, darkness covers the earth,
     and thick darkness is over the peoples;
But the Lord rises upon you,
     and his glory appears over you" (Is 60:1-2).

This was the first Scripture given me when I was baptized in the Spirit in the Fall of 1969. It is still very life-giving for me to know the call to rise and shine for the glory of the Lord will rise upon me. No matter how much of the glory I have experienced I know there is more.

"For the Lord will be your everlasting light and your God shall be your glory" (Is 60:19).

God of Zion, great God, Holy God, all your great prophets experienced and spoke of the glory of God. I, too, in Your time have come to experience Your glory. I want to praise and thank You today for every big and little experience of Your glory. "Rise up in splendor in my life. . . . Your light has come." Continue and complete the work that You have begun in me for the glory of the Father.

79

RAINBOWS OF GLORY

Like the appearance of a rainbow in the clouds on a rainy day, so was the radiance around Him. This was the appearance of the likeness of the glory of the Lord. When I saw it, I fell facedown, and I heard the voice of one speaking.

(Ez 1:28)

IN THE BOOK OF EZEKIEL, the prophet provides us many descriptions of the Lord's glory.

"Then the glory of the Lord rose from above the cherubim and moved to the threshold of the temple. The cloud filled the temple, and the court was full of the radiance of the glory of the Lord" (Ez 10:4).

"And I saw the glory of the God of Israel coming from the east. His voice was like the roar of rushing waters, and the land was radiant with His glory" (Ez 43:2).

"Then the Spirit lifted me up and brought me into the inner court and the glory of the Lord filled the temple" (Ez 43:5).

Today I am recalling something I experienced a short time after my Baptism in the Holy Spirit. A pastor from an interfaith group was sharing and praying a bit with me. He ended with saying: "Get into the Word, Sister. Get into the Word."

My unexpressed thought was: "It is such a big book. I read it once." At that time, I did not even own my own Bible. We were not supposed to have superfluous things. My thought was: "I read it once. If I ever want to re-read it, I could always get one from the library."

That night I had a very vivid dream. I was at a party. The announcement was made: "The prize goes to Sister Francis Clare."

The prize was a scroll. In my dream, I questioned: "Do I eat it all at once or a page at a time?"

With that I awoke, found a Bible, cracked it open for a word, and there it was: the dream about eating the scroll. "He said to me: Son of man, eat what is before you; eat this scroll, then go, speak to the house of Israel. So I opened my mouth and He gave me the scroll to eat. Son of man, He then said to me, feed your belly and fill your stomach with this scroll I am giving you. I ate it, and it was as sweet as honey in my mouth. He said: Son of man, go now to the house of Israel, and speak my words to them" (Ez 3:1-4) (NAB).

Lord God, send rainbows of Your glory into our lives—rainbows of Your love and Your promises to be with us always. Speak to us as You did to Your prophets in dreams and visions in the night. Flood our hearts as You did Ezekiel's temple with the radiance of Your glory, now and forever. Amen.

80

FUTURE GLORY GREATER

For thus says the Lord of hosts: One moment yet, a little while, and I will shake the heavens and the earth, the sea and the dry land. I will shake all the nations and the treasures of all the nations will come in, And I will fill the house with glory, says the Lord of hosts. Mine is the silver and mine the gold says the Lord of hosts. Greater will be the future glory of this house than the former, says the Lord of hosts, And in this place I will give you peace, says the Lord of hosts.

(Hg 2:6-9)

WHAT IS "one moment yet?"

What is "a little while?"

With God "a thousand years are like a day and a day is like a thousand years."

Dare we limit the mystery and the meaning of God's eternal Word by putting a single literal interpretation on it and thereby forever rob God's people of the full and timeless meaning of the words?

This we know that our God will fill this house that is our Church, our family, our nation, our individual lives with a future glory much greater than the former.

"Who are you to say 'Enough! Enough!'

when I your God say 'There is more! There is more!'

There is MORE I would reveal to you,

MORE I would pour out upon you for I am a God of
    surprises!

Eye has not seen nor ear heard nor has it entered the
    heart of man to dream what God has prepared for
    those who love Me.

These are not idle words.

I who spoke them will bring them to pass.

Come to know Me as a God of surprises even now!"

Oh God, what a mighty God we serve! You are a God of surprises! We welcome even now the surprise You have in store for us tomorrow, next week, next month, next year. We welcome the surprise for the new millennium. Give us a new heart and a new mind that all You desire to give us can be contained in it.

81

RADIANCE OF GOD'S GLORY

**All of us, gazing with unveiled faces on the glory of
the Lord, are being transformed into the same image
from glory to glory, as from the Lord who is the Spirit.**

(2 Cor 3:18) (NAB)

AS YOU AWAKE IN THE MORNING, know the whole earth is full of His glory.

The glory of the Annunciation, Christmas glory, Taboric glory, glory of the Resurrection, all are waiting to be liberated in us.

The whole earth is full of His glory. What about you? Are you full of His glory? Glory is the fruit of His life in us. What blocks the glory for you? What releases the glory in you? We are one with Jesus. He is one with us.

"The Son is the radiance of God's glory and the exact representation of his being, sustaining all things by his powerful word. After he had provided purification for sins, he sat down at the right hand of the Majesty in heaven" (Heb 1:3).

While we await His Second Coming, let us live in the glory of His First Coming!

"And when the Chief Shepherd appears, you will receive the crown of glory that will never fade away" (1 Pt 5:4).

Precious God, yes we are being transformed from light to light, grace to grace, glory to glory. We are way down the road from where we were when we first began praying through Your message on glory. We have crossed our Rubicon. There is no turning back, only GOING FORWARD!

While we await that Second Coming of our Lord, Jesus Christ, grace us, O God, to live in the glory of the First Coming!

82

SOLOMON IN ALL HIS GLORY

Why are you anxious about clothes? Learn from the way the wild flowers grow. They do not work or spin. But I tell you that not even Solomon in all of his glory was clothed like one of them.

(Mt 6:29)

JESUS TEACHES US dependence on God the Father. Your heavenly Father knows all that you need. Seek first the kingdom of God which is coming soon and very soon, and all these other things will be given you besides. Do not be anxious about tomorrow.

Your God is saying: "Do not be anxious." The same God who said: "Do not commit adultery." One we take seriously, the other we say: "But I have all these reasons to be anxious."

"Do not be anxious," Jesus says.

It is an absolute No-No! So what are you going to do about it today?

Tomorrow will take care of itself! Tomorrow we look forward to Jesus coming in great power and glory! "Sufficient for the day is its own evil," Jesus says.

Jesus would not have us full of fear for tomorrow. He would have us trusting the heavenly Father, who clothes the lilies of the field and the birds of the air, to take care of us. Many people today question whether we need to store things for the difficult times ahead.

The answer is: "Your heavenly Father knows that you need them. Seek first the kingdom of God and his righteousness and all these things will be given you besides" (Mt 6:33) (NAB).

Do you really believe it? Or is it a "tongue in cheek" word for you?

Jesus, lift from our hearts the root cause of all anxiety no matter what the cause. Forgive us for all the times we have allowed anxiety to root itself in our hearts and our spirits. Forgive all the times we have made decisions rooted in the anxiety of our minds and hearts. Help us to seek first Your Kingdom so that we may know on a very real, gutsy level that all other good things will be given to us besides by Our Father in heaven.

83

THINE THE KINGDOM, THE POWER, THE GLORY

To him who loves us and has freed us from our sins by his blood . . . to him be glory and power forever and ever.

(Rv 1:5-6) (NAB)

THERE IS A GREAT WAVE of power that goes forth, great
      waves of power that you do not see because you
      are too small to see.
I would have you see these waves of power as you
      gaze into My Heart.
My love for you is sufficient cause for rejoicing
      without seeing the results.
I am setting you on the crest of the wave that you may
      ride with Me and I want you to enjoy it!

The Lord is speaking to me after a hard frustrating after-
noon in which idea after idea of how I thought He would work
fell by the wayside. I set about to organize all the Scriptures on
glory from the New Testament. The feel was like ashes in the
mouth! No power! No anointing! I finally asked, "Jesus, do you
really want me to do this?"

The answer was quick and simple: "No, not really!"

I tried praying for a very special outpouring of the Holy
Spirit. Then waited for some great revelation of how He would
have me organize all that I had received for that book.

Nothing! Absolutely nothing came! Feeling very fatigued, I
allowed myself time to sleep. Still no idea for the next move.

Perhaps a little food, a cup of tea would help. No change!

Jesus, I am ready for an Isaiah anointing. Ready for You to
show me how You are going to use me in magnificence and
glory. Nothing! No word! No message! Nothing to lift me up.

Nothing to direct my thinking or to set my feet on a right path.

In utter frustration, I finally went on my face before my Jesus crucified and cried out: "God, I am listening."

"When you get too big, too organized, needing to control, I cannot use you. I need you to stay little and simple before Me."

"But Jesus, it is so hard."

"I need you to stay little and simple before Me."

"Okay, God, I will! Put me on Your Potter's Wheel. Change my left brain to right. Work on my brain, on my faith imagination, whatever needs to be worked on, I give you permission." Before I let go entirely I needed to say, "Oh, I am so ready to help You out, to give You a million ideas."

"Franny, My bride, I don't need a million ideas. I just need you to hear what My one idea is. The book is for My glory and it will be birthed in My time. I know you have not yet begun, but you are finished! There is nothing you can do except receive. Know that it is I desiring to use you, not you desiring to use Me."

O God, You are so right! I keep forgetting that Your thoughts are above my thoughts like the heavens are above the earth. That is far! Far! Far! I yield every aspect of this writing to You, Lord Jesus. Let that great wave of power come over me, to touch and to change my brain and my heart. At Your invitation, I will arise to ride the crest of the wave. I will keep my gaze on Your heart. There I choose to enjoy every precious wild moment of today's journey.

84

THRONE OF GLORY

And then they will see the Son of Man coming in a cloud with power and great glory. But when these signs begin to happen, stand erect and raise your heads because your redemption is at hand.

(Lk 21:27-28) (NAB)

JESUS WOULD SAY TO US TODAY, what would it profit us if we gained the whole world, if we became the richest person in the world and had all the resources in the world, what would it profit us if we lost our eternal life?

"For the Son of Man will come with his angels in his Father's glory and then he will repay everyone according to his conduct" (Mt 16:27) (NAB).

I believe that this is going to happen very soon. The Son of Man, Jesus, will come with His angels in His Father's glory. We will see Him in His glory! In your prayer time today rejoice in that word. Cry out from the very depths of your being, "Come, Lord Jesus with Your angels in Your Father's glory. Repay everyone according to their conduct. Come, Lord Jesus with Your angels in Your Father's glory! Come!"

We read in the Gospel of Matthew, the story of the rich young man and Jesus' response to him: "If you wish to be perfect, go sell what you have and give to the poor and you will have treasure in heaven. Then come, follow me. When the young man heard this statement, he went away sad, for he had many possessions. Then Jesus said to his disciples, 'Amen I say to you, it will be hard for one who is rich to enter the kingdom of heaven. Again I say to you it is easier for a camel to pass through the eye of a needle than for one who is rich to enter the kingdom of God.' When the disciples heard this they were greatly astonished and said, 'Who then can be saved?' Jesus looked at them and said, 'For human beings this is impossible but for God all things are possible.' Then Peter said to him in reply, 'We have given up everything and followed you. What will there be for us?' Jesus said to them, 'Amen I say to you that you who have followed me, in the new age, when the Son of Man is seated on his throne of glory will yourselves sit on twelve thrones, judging the twelve tribes of Israel'" (Mt 19:21-28) (NAB).

Jesus would say to us as He said to Peter and to His apostles, "Amen I say to you that you who have followed Me in this time when the Son of Man is seated on His Throne of glory you too will be seated there."

We, too, will share that Throne of glory with everyone who has given up houses, brothers, sisters, father, mother, children or lands for the sake of His Name and will receive a hundred times more and will inherit eternal life.

This is God's promise! This is our security! All of us who have given up wealth, brothers, sisters, whatever for the sake of the Kingdom will receive a hundredfold and will inherit Eternal Life forever and ever. Glory!

We thank You, Lord Jesus, for the gift of Eternal Life. We thank You that You will soon come in glory. We praise You that You are seated on your Throne of glory, not just with the twelve apostles. You will share that Throne of glory with each of us, forever and ever and ever.

Jesus, this is mystery beyond our understanding but we say yes to the mystery! What a future is in store for us to share Your Throne of glory forever and ever!

85

ONLY THE FATHER'S GLORY

**Today, if you should hear God's voice, do not harden
your hearts as in the rebellion.**

(Heb 3:15) (AIV)

**For if Jesus had given them rest, God did not speak
later about another day. So then, sabbath rest still
remains for the people of God; for those who enter
God's rest cease from their labors as God also did. Let
us therefore make every effort to enter that rest.**

(Heb 4:8-11) (AIV)

"MY CHOSEN PEOPLE never entered into their rest. Today you are
being called into that Hebrew rest so that We can do a work in
you and through you to bring about the Father's glory."

For a long time I settled for just stillness, waiting, not doing
a thing. It got boring, so I checked out a few left-brained ideas,
but there was no response on God's part.

I again thought of organizing all the Scriptures on glory.
What an impressive thing that could be!

"But I am not asking you to do that," I heard the Father say.
"You are asked to receive a book, not to write one. To receive a
devotional, not write one. I will give it to you word for word,
thought for thought, paragraph for paragraph. I will dictate it to
you even as I dictated the Ten Commandments to Moses on Mt.
Sinai. I will give it to you. You can trust Me. It will be from Me
and it will be for My glory."

"Checking down in the deepest part of you, Franny, My
bride. I see that secret desire to come back to Milwaukee, and
have just a little tinge of glory. 'I am back! See folks, I have done
it! Here it is! I have been before God and this is what He said.'
Right?"

"Right, God!"

"Own your sinfulness. Own that thread, that pattern that

has so often been there to sneak a little bit of My glory. You have been put down by many that love you and some who don't. So sneaking just a little bit of My glory could make you feel better. I am saying to you today as I have said to you before, this is not the way to go for you or for any of My people. I will not share My glory with anyone!"

Okay, God! Okay! To You be the Glory for all that is and for all that will be. If Your Mother Mary could give to You all the glory for the way that You used her to bring about the salvation of the world, then, with Your grace, I can surely let go of any need for glory in doing this work today.

"God who is mighty has done great things for me. Holy is his name" (Lk 1:49) (NAB).

GLORY BE YOURS FOREVER

Humble yourself before the Lord, and he will lift you up.

(Jas 4:10) (NJB)

I AM ABOUT AS LOW as I can get, prostrate on the floor in my prayer room. It feels good! It feels like here is the place where my God can reach me. He can lift me up! And I can lift Him up.

Jesus says: "And when I am lifted up from the earth, I will draw everyone to myself" (Jn 12:32) (NAB).

On this holy rug, with my face to the ground, with my hands stretched out, I cry out: "I lift You up, Lord Jesus! Do whatever You want. Speak whatever You want to speak for Your people. Teach them as You are teaching me that if they want to go from glory to glory, it is not by being high and lifted up, it is in being low and lowly before You.

There You will find them. You will reach them. You will speak to them. As they are willing to be lowly before You, You will lift them up into glory! You will use them mightily to ready Your people for Your Coming in Glory! For the kingdom, the power and the glory are Yours! Now and forever!

In 1984 I was called to speak at a youth conference in Germany. The theme was "If I Be Lifted Up I Will Draw All People to Myself." As we prayed in a healing service for more than three hours, all we did was to lift up Jesus and instantly one after the other some 1,200 youth rested in the Spirit for the healing and empowering they needed.

Lord Jesus, we have the perfect example of humility in Your life and death. You humbled Yourself in becoming obedient even unto death that we might have life, eternal life with You. Grant us the grace to be humble before You. We thank You for the price You paid that we might some day be lifted up into eternal glory.

HONOR AND GLORY FOREVER

**God greatly exalted him and bestowed on him the
name that is above every other name, that at the name
of Jesus, every knee shall bow and every tongue
confess that Jesus Christ is Lord, to the glory of the
Father.**

(Phil 2:9-11)

**Now to the king eternal, immortal, invisible, the only
God, be honor and glory forever and ever. Amen.**

(1 Tim 1:17)

JESUS HAS SAID TO ME I have many things to teach you about glory.
One is in Chapter 4 of Matthew. "The devil took Me up to a very
high mountain and showed Me all the kingdoms of the world in
their glory. He said to Me, 'All these I will give to You if You will
prostrate Yourself and worship me.'

"I said to him, 'Get away, Satan.' It is written, 'The Lord Your
God shall you worship and Him alone shall you serve.' And then
the devil left Me. And behold angels came and ministered to Me.

"Today I would say to My people, 'Learn from Me how to
deal with the temptation to pile up the kingdoms of this world
and all their magnificence. Learn to say 'Get away, Satan. It is
written the Lord your God shall you worship, and Him alone
shall you serve.'"

Jesus has a further word for us about how to deal with
glory and praise, "When you give alms, do not blow a trumpet
before you as the hypocrites do in the synagogues and in the
streets to win the praise of others. Amen, I say to you, they have
received their reward. But when you give alms do not let your
left hand know what your right is doing, so that your almsgiving
may be secret. And your Father who sees in secret will repay
you" (Mt 6:2) (NAB). He will repay you with a share of the glory
that is in His kingdom.

Very soon you will have a measure of glory for every time you have given in His name!

We humble ourselves under Your mighty hand, O God. If only we could see what You see and know what You know, how differently we would live our lives. Open our eyes, our ears, our mouths, all of our senses that we may be Your people and You may be our God!

88

THE FATHER'S GLORY

If anyone is ashamed of me and of my words in this adulterous and sinful generation, the Son of Man will be ashamed of him when he comes in his Father's glory with the holy angels.

(Mk 8:38)

HOW GLAD WE WILL BE a few years from now when we too stand in that Holy Place, that we have not been ashamed of Jesus and His words. So neither will Jesus "be ashamed of us when He comes in His Father's glory with the holy angels." In fact He will be proud of us! He will be proud that we in this time of a faithless and sinful generation have been willing to stand up and be a disciple of Jesus.

What delight then can we take today when it costs us something not to be ashamed of Jesus or His words. What delight we can take as we share our belief in Jesus and His words with those who are faithless and sinful. We can know that when Jesus comes in His Father's glory with all the holy angels He will be proud of us for the witness that we have borne Him today. He will be proud that we have been willing to witness to His gospel.

The fact is that He will soon come in His Father's glory with all His holy angels. Has your heart ever really cried out, "Come, Lord Jesus in Your Father's glory with all Your holy angels as You have promised You would. Come, Lord Jesus, in great power and glory!"

We realize that we are not too much different than James and John in their ambition as they said to Jesus:

"'Teacher, we want you to do for us whatever we ask of you.' He replied, 'What do you wish me to do for you?' They answered him, 'Grant that in your glory we may sit one at your right and the other at your left.'

"Jesus said, 'You do not know what you are asking. Can you drink the cup that I drink or be baptized with the baptism with which I am baptized?' They said, 'We can.' Jesus said, 'The cup that I give you will drink, and with the baptism with which I am baptized, you will be baptized, but to sit at my right or at my left is not mine to give, but is for those for whom it has been prepared by my Father.'

"When the ten heard this, they became indignant at James and John. Jesus summoned them and said, 'You know that those who are recognized as rulers over the Gentiles lord it over them and their great ones make their authority over them felt. But it shall not be so among you. Rather whoever wishes to be great among you will be your servant; and whoever wishes to be first among you will be the slave of all. For the Son of Man did not come to be served, but to serve and to give his life as a ransom for many'" (Mk 10:35-45) (NAB).

Jesus, thank You for calling us as You did James and John to be among Your faithful followers. Show us today what it means to take up our cross and follow You. There is much we need to learn about being one of Your faithful followers. Teach us by the power of Your Holy Spirit. Equip us with strong faith in You and Your teachings so that we may never be ashamed of You or Your words.

We look forward to the time when You will come in Your Father's glory together with all Your holy angels. Come, Lord Jesus, in great power and glory!

89

ALL GLORY BE YOURS FOREVER

**May the God of peace, who brought back from the
dead our Lord Jesus Christ, the great shepherd of the
sheep, by the blood of the eternal covenant, make you
complete in everything good, so that you may do
God's will. Working among us that which is pleasing
in God's sight, through Jesus Christ, to whom be
glory forever and ever. Amen.**

(Heb 13:20-21) (AIV)

EVERY JOURNEY has its landmarks. The 25th of August was a land-
mark for me. I finished a work God had called me to do—praying through all the Scriptures on glory. I had been moved with
them, blessed with them, filled with them, freed with them.
Finally I arrived at a place where I was saying, "But Lord, what
do I do with what You have done in me. What am I called to do?
How am I called to organize this?"

I sat before the Lord in my prayer time, with a blank sheet
of paper before me, saying "Lord, I have done everything You
have shown me. I have followed the lead of your Spirit day by
day, hour by hour, task by task. What do You want me to do? I
have no idea how You will use all this for the book You have
spoken about. Here I am today with a blank sheet of paper.

"The paper is blank until You put something on it. Until You
show me by the power of Your Spirit, how to organize and what
to organize, I am a blank."

For a long, long, long time I was quiet. No thought was
coming. Nothing was happening. My best prayer registered:
"Lord, I am a blank until You speak."

As time went on, I spoke variations of the facts: "Lord, it is
blankety blank! Do you see what I see? Nothing, Lord! Nothing!
Do you hear what I hear? Nothing, Lord! Nothing!" More time
dragged by. That was one thing I had plenty of—time! I perse-
vered in waiting on a silent God.

Suddenly like a lightning flash the thought hit me—a devotional! A devotional! A devotional entitled *Glory to Glory!*

A devotional! Why, that's what Servant Publishers through David Came asked for two years ago. What a confirmation!

"I will give to you a devotional for My people to show them day by day, hour by hour, task by task, how to be transformed from glory to glory. That's why I took you through some four hundred Glory Scriptures—to prepare you for a devotional!"

With that the humor of it all hit me. "And You knew it all the time. A devotional! Of course, all this could best fit in a devotional."

My first temptation was to go to a Christian bookstore to check out "devotionals." If I am going to write one, I had better read one. I had best know the what, when, where, why and how of them.

Before I could do this, the Lord checked me with: "I am not asking you to write one, I am asking you to receive one."

Lord God, Father, Son, and Holy Spirit, what can I say but yes. Be it done according to Your word and Your promise. I humble myself before Your plan for a devotional for Your people. Use me in whatever way You see fit. May all glory be Yours forever and ever. Amen.

90

MANIFEST YOUR GLORY

It will burst into bloom; it will rejoice greatly and shout for joy. The glory of Lebanon will be given to it, the splendor of Carmel and Sharon; they will see the glory of the Lord, the splendor of our God.

(Is 35:2)

And the glory of the Lord will be revealed, and all mankind together will see it. For the mouth of the Lord has spoken.

(Is 40:5)

AUGUST 26 WAS A DAY when I was so hungry for the manifestation of the glory of God that I actually wept in my morning prayer. As I took down my picture of Jesus coming in glory, I said, "I don't want a picture anymore. I want a manifestation. I want to see You in Your power. I want to see You in Your glory. Surely there is some way that you can manifest Yourself to me."

As I did this I caught Jesus saying, "Allow everything today to be a manifestation of My love for you. The cup of coffee you are about to perk. Let it be a sign of My love for you. Instead of a health drink, let Me treat you to a real breakfast: Toast, an egg, and cantaloupe. All a sign of My love for you."

As I sat down to eat, I was moved to tears. I realized that this was the first time since I arrived here that I had wept out of pure loneliness for people with skin on. I had just spent twenty-seven days alone with my God!

Precious God, Father, Son, and Holy Spirit, only You know all the journeys and the yearnings of my heart in these past weeks. Only You know how vast a vacuum I still hold inside me that can only be filled with a deeper, richer, "beyond"

experience of the Living God. Only You know the plans You have for me when I move on from this prayer time. I say "Yes" to whatever way You would lead me so that You may reveal Yourself to me in the glory of our Father.

I choose to believe that I will see the glory of the Lord, the splendor of our God, as I continue to walk on in faith, trust and love.

And I choose to allow everything that happens to me today to be a manifestation of Your love. Everything beautiful, everything wonderful, everything holy and precious will have a card attached that says: "With love from your God."

91

SURPRISES OF GLORY

**Let us rejoice and be glad and give him glory! For the
wedding day of the Lamb has come, and his bride has
made herself ready.**

(Rv 19:7)

ON THE 27TH, I awakened to what seemed to be the middle of the
night. In reality it was early, early morning.

I knew that this was the day in which I was being called to
a 4:00 a.m. rising to spend time with Jesus, my Bridegroom, the
Father, and the Holy Spirit. I intended spending an extended
time in prayer—perhaps three hours, like my Bridegroom spent
upon the cross. From that cross I would receive the energy, the
victory, the inspiration to receive all that God wanted me to
receive. As always I began my day with proclaiming Jesus as
Lord.

As I came out of my sleep with many "Ho hums," I wondered if I was really awake enough to discern and say yes to a
still small voice. I decided to believe it. The Scripture for the day
was Elijah in 1Kings 19:11-13. God was not in the wind, the earthquake, the fire, but in 'the sound of sheer silence.' It was all
around me! Sheer silence!

I allowed myself to listen to the Scripture again. When I
heard it I, too, wrapped my face in my mantle, went out, and
stood at the entrance to my cottage cave. I listened to the roaring
of the ocean waves, the wind, and the sound of "sheer silence."

I knew that I had three special days left. So I designated one
for the Father! One for the Son! One for the Holy Spirit! And all
three for all three!

Like Philip, I said to Jesus: "Show me the Father and it is
enough." Jesus said to me as to Philip, "Have you been with Me
this long and you still do not realize that the Father and I are one?
Whoever sees Me sees the Father."

"Oh yes," I said, "I see You in my faith imagination. I see You in that picture on the wall in the glory of Your Resurrection. I see Your nail-scarred hands stretched out to me. Your eyes sparkling! You are telling me that You have surprises for me this day and that I'll never guess what or how many."

"The first surprise is 'I want to take you by the hand and lead you to the Father. So close your eyes and get into that wedding step and I, Your Bridegroom, will walk you, My bride, down the aisle up to My Father's Throne on this morning of August 27, 1993.'"

I walked with my arm in the arm of Jesus right up to the Throne that I might be presented to the Father. As I walked, the joy within me began to deepen and to swell until I thought I would explode with joy.

I realized that the real world is not the world that I see with my physical eyes, that I hear with my physical ears, but it is the world of the supernatural! For me the real world is step by step to be walking up to that Throne on the arm of Jesus to be presented to the Father.

The real world is to see the Father, like I have never seen Him, to hear His voice as I have never heard it, to give my love to Him like I have never before been able. The real world is in my faith imagination to stand in His awesome presence. The real world is to hear the voice of Jesus singing in the background:

"Here comes the bride,
All beautiful inside.
Oh how I love
My beautiful, beautiful bride."

It was our song from that first night of my three-month stay at Cape Cod when the Shekinah Glory came down. I allowed myself again just to bask in that glory in a timeless space and place.

Gradually, I realized that it was Jesus singing and His bride was not just me but Jesus was singing about the beauty in the bride that is my community, my church, and the churches of the world. He was singing of the beauty in His bride, the people of the world, the churched and the unchurched. He was singing about a bride that He saw with His eternal vision.

The heavenly choir was singing "As I Stand in Thy Presence." I dared not doubt the reality of that Presence! So real! So full of light! So full of glory!

As I stood there, I was clothed in the righteousness of Jesus. That is my wedding gown: His righteousness! Nothing about me is better than anyone else. There is no merit on my own part. I opened my Scripture to Revelations 19.

"A voice coming from the throne said: 'Praise our God, all you his servants, [and] you who revere him, small and great.'

Then I heard something like a sound of a great multitude or the sound of rushing water or mighty peals of thunder, as they said:

'Alleluia!'

Alleluia the Lord has established his reign, [our] God, the Almighty. Let us rejoice and be glad and give him glory.

For the wedding day of the Lamb has come, his bride has made herself ready. She was allowed to wear a bright, clean linen garment.

(The linen represents the righteous deeds of the holy ones.)

Then the angel said to me, 'Write this: Blessed are those who have been called to the wedding feast of the Lamb.' And He said to me, 'These words are true; they come from God.'" (Rv 19:5-9) (NAB).

It is all God's doing! "He who is mighty has done great things for me. Holy is his name" (Lk 1:49) (NAB).

Father, holy is Your name, for You have done great things in me. Holy is Your name! Greater yet will You do in each one of us as we continue to believe and to grow in our relationship with You.

Father, this is a, "Your Move God Day!" Move us with giant strides into a deeper and deeper love relationship and into Kingdom living!

92

UNFADING GLORY

**Now the Lord is the Spirit, and where the Spirit of the
Lord is, there is freedom. All of us, gazing with
unveiled faces on the glory of the Lord, are being
transformed into the same image from glory to glory
as from the Lord who is the Spirit.**

(2 Cor 3:17-18) (NAB)

"NOW IF THE MYSTERY OF DEATH, carved in letters on stone, was so
glorious that the Israelites could not look intently on the face of
Moses because of its glory that was going to fade, how much
more will the ministry of the Spirit be glorious. For if the ministry
of condemnation was glorious, the ministry of righteousness will
abound much more in glory. Indeed, what was endowed with
glory has come to have no glory in this respect because of the
glory that surpasses it. For if what was going to fade was glorious, how much more will what endures be glorious" (2 Cor 3:7-
11) (NAB).

"Now the Lord is a Spirit, and where the Spirit of the Lord
is, there is freedom. All of us, gazing with unveiled faces on the
glory of the Lord, are being transformed into the same image
from glory to glory as from the Lord who is the Spirit" (2 Cor
3:18) (NAB). And this is God's Word! We cannot hear it too often
or drink too deeply of its meaning for each one of us.

In today's Scripture we have the key to our own day by day,
hour by hour, minute by minute, task by task transformation into
God's very image. What more could anyone ask, hope for or
desire?

*Lord Jesus, allow me to understand like I have never
understood before that You are a God of glory and that Your
glory unlike that of Moses will never fade. Yours is the
surpassing glory which will endure forever. Such is the glory*

that we attribute to You every time we pray the Great Doxology: "Glory be to the Father, and to the Son, and to the Holy Spirit." This is the unfading, unsurpassing glory that we are being transformed into by the Spirit that we will share with You for all eternity.

Grant me the grace in the now to unceasingly gaze on Your glory that I may according to Your word be transformed more and more into Your likeness by the power and the working of Your Holy Spirit. Amen and Amen.

93

THE FATHER

IT IS EARLY, early morning on the 28th. I am beginning to hear the swishing sounds of Hawaii's cars zooming on the North Shore Highway. The world is coming alive out of the night's darkness. How glad I am to be moving out of my own darkness into the morning of God's glory!

Across the room I see my August calendar. Three days to go in my Kamehameha Prayer Pantry! Today is the day designated for the Father.

With that dawning I swing out of bed onto my knees declaring, "Jesus, You are the Lord of this new day designated for Your Father."

"Our Father!" Jesus corrected me.

"Our Father it is! Thank You, Jesus!" I let the 'our' sink deep, deep, deep into my awakening heart. "And what is our Father's agenda today?"

"The Father wants you to know how much He loves
     you."

"How do I love you?

I love you with an everlasting love with a father and a
     mother's love from all eternity.

From your mother's womb I have called you by name.

I love you with a forgiving love, a creative love, an
     effective love.

I love you not because of who you are but because of
     who I called you to be, not for what you would
     make of yourself but for what I would make of
     you, not because you never fail Me but because
     even in those failures I can redeem you and love
     you.

How do I love you?

I love you with the same love I have for Jesus.

I cannot love you more than I do.

I love you with an enabling love so that you can truly
     say to Me, Father, I love you too!"

"Father, I love You, too!" Sitting on the floor in my prayer pantry I was enabled to say it again and again and again with ever deeper meaning. "Father, I love You, too! Father, I love You, too! Father, I love You, too! More today than yesterday, but not as much as tomorrow and certainly not as much as I will love You for all eternity!

"Father, I desire to respond to Your love on every level on which You have loved me from all eternity. I do not claim to understand such love in You or in me, but I choose to say yes to it. I choose to live my life more and more in a manner worthy of such love."

There was no timing anything in my Hawaii stay-away, there was just the eternal NOW to move with God's agenda.

So after God's "while", the Father invited me to sit at my kitchen-table Throne. "I am so glad that you are here," He said, "so that we can just talk. So we can be intimate friends like Moses was with Me."

As I looked into His eyes, I wondered how I could have lived this long without desiring with all my heart, with all my soul, with all my being, to let go of everything else so I might know My Father in the way that He is known.

In the days I had been here, I often opened *Your Move, God*, when I needed to hear from the Father. The right word was always there. My Father speaking directly to me saying exactly what I needed to hear: "You are two in one, Bridegroom and bride in the heart of your Father" spoke the truth more than any other word. It affirmed who I was, where I was, and what I was about.

"Rejoice to be like a little child and you will come to know the bigness of your God" was another word that was key to my knowing what God was doing and what God wanted to do. If there was anything that could block my journey of intimacy with God, it was my need to be big, when God was simply calling me to be little.

I spent countless hours talking to my Abba, my Daddy, my Papa. In my prayer language, I could tell Him in ways I never could in English, how great He is, how wonderful, how good, and how holy! It was like living through the best movie I had ever seen involving the greatest actors, actresses, plot, and drama. To say more would be to say too much.

What I can say is: I said yes to whatever the Father was doing in my life, in the lives of my family, my church, my order, my nation, and my world. I said yes to the call that is on our lives to live in a loving relationship with the Father who is full of glory.

In many ways it was a fun and games time. There were times when I realized that I could allow myself to be touched by little trickles or allow the vast ocean surf to wash over me again and again. To settle for the trickle or to invite the whole ocean to flow over me was like a mini-glory-game. Invariably the big splash won out over the little trickle!

Snatches of poetry kept me in God's Presence. Like Gerard Manley Hopkins' poem, "Thee, God":

Thee, God, I come from, to thee go,
All day long I like fountain flow
From out thy hand.

Over and over the refrain rose and fell like the ocean waves. Whatever else was happening I felt like the richest kid on the block.

"To be one with Me means to lose yourself in the heart of your Father so that we are no longer two but just one." I learned from Jesus how to lose myself in the heart of My Father. I learned from Him how to pray "Our Father who art in heaven."

"My child, for almost two thousand years, My Son has been praying for this oneness that you may be one in Me as Jesus was one in Me. I promise you that we will be one."

As the day went by I received word after word. "Never fear when the time is over it will all be there in your mind and in your spirit. All you need to know you will know. All you need to become you will have become. Allow yourself to absorb the depth, the height, the length, and the breadth of your Father's love and it will happen."

Sometimes I needed to hear other words like: "Hands off means hands off so I can get My hands on." or "Who's asking you to do that?"

I would realize it was the "old Fran" and I would let go. Sometimes a thing was half done when I realized that this was something that God was not asking me to do. It could be as basic as one hand manicured and the other not. I realized in the middle of a task that God was not asking me to do that now. He was asking something else. The test was whether I could let go of my agenda for His.

"I demand absolute obedience. Delayed obedience is disobedience." It has been quite an experience, allowing myself in love to be disciplined by My Father. In the power of the Holy Spirit, I learned to enjoy it. It did not happen overnight nor was it the fruit of just one prayer time.

"Oh, that's what you're asking! You don't want me to do this? Okay, Father!"

"Know that I am God, not you. Listen to Me, My child, and with the listening will come light. Out of light will come direction and strength, as you enter into My rest, you will enter into My eternal activity. You are to fast not only from food, but from needing to fully understand."

My greatest fast was from needing to fully understand. There was much I did not understand. I just needed to let go and let God, to believe that my Father was at work.

"There is much I desire to teach you about the great mystery of love. All eternity is not long enough. When you are totally surrendered to My life, it is finished. The rest is up to Me."

I know that I am not totally surrendered yet. Having a month like this only helped me to realize in how many areas I am not surrendered. I am still in charge! To let the Father be Father! That is what this process has been! To let go and let God!

"Unless the grain of wheat fall into the ground and die, itself remains alone" (Jn 12:24). My choice, and I often needed to come back to it, was to be the grain of wheat buried. My prayer was that even more than the discipline, I might experience the love of my Father. I asked to be clothed in love, wrapped in love, imbued with love, totally loved by my Father.

I opened myself in a very special way for a new infilling of the Holy Spirit, that the Spirit might reveal to me the Father's love. I prayed for an ongoing revelation of the Father's love with each step I take, each beautiful view that I see, each sound I listen to—like the chirping of the cricket out there, the sloshing of the waves, the movement of the palm trees. All was a "God-mark" card from my Father, saying "I love you. You are My child. I love you. You are the bride for My Son. I love you."

I remember the day the Father said, "Allow Me to love you in a thousand ways every day." So I am saying today "Father, I am not only allowing You to love me, I am begging You to love me. I desire to experience that love, to feel that love, to sing out that love in new songs and old."

I sang out for the heavens and the ocean to take note:

"The Father loves me this I know, for the Spirit tells me so.
Little ones to Him belong. We are weak, but He is strong.
Yes, the Father loves me, Yes, the Father loves me,
Yes, the Father loves me, the Spirit tells me so."

"Come, Holy Spirit, to my Kamehameha Prayer Pantry" was the cry of my heart! "Come with a mighty wind and tongues of fire like you filled that Upper Room. Come reveal to me today how much my Father loves me."

"All day long, on this special day in honor of Your Father I have been with you. I have heard you pray: 'I am here for You!' Now hear Me say: 'I AM here for you!' I have been ready to speak and you have been readied to listen. I AM as close to you as your next thought and as close to you as the tears that I have seen you shedding out of pure desire to hear from Me. I AM as close to you as the very breath you breathe.

"I AM your Father who brought you into existence that you might love Me. I have created you that you might know My love, as Abraham knew it, as Isaac, Jacob, and Moses, My intimate friends knew it. I brought you into existence that you might know My love and My glory as the great Patriarchs and Saints of the Old and New Testament knew it.

"I brought you here that you might know the longing that I have in My heart to be for you a God who is Intimate Friend and Lover. How I longed that My Chosen People might enter into that bridal relationship that I am calling you into. But somehow in spite of all the graces, the gifts, the power, the manifestations of My glory, in spite of all the times that I forgave them, called them back, renewed them, restored them, even brought them into the Promised Land, in spite of all that, they never came to know My bridal love for them. I was never able to consummate the marriage. The desire that I had to bring My Chosen People into a bridal union with their Father, their Creator, their Lord has never been fulfilled.

"So in this new time under this New Covenant, in these End Times in which you are living, I rejoice that My people, the people I have formed, as I formed My Chosen People in the Old Testament, the people I have formed under the Lordship of Jesus, to enter into the bridal relationship that I will reveal to you.

"I will reveal to you My glory and My love which I was never able to reveal to My Chosen People in the Old Testament. I rejoice to call you into that intimate relationship that I called My

Son, Jesus. I rejoice to be able to spend days and nights with you on the mountaintop as I did with Jesus. I rejoice to call you into that hidden life and beyond it.

"This is a time in which your tears are joined with Mine. They are tears of joy, tears of fulfillment, which were first in the heart and in the eyes of My Son as He cried for you in times of prayer on the hillside and on the seaside of Galilee. My Son cried for you in the Garden that you might enter into the glory that was prepared for you in a relationship that My Chosen People of the Old Testament never knew.

"Oh My precious, precious sons and daughters, you are being called in this time to share the glory that was meant for My Chosen People from all time. You are being called to share the glory that was manifested time and time again, the glory that is in Me from all eternity. There is mystery in that glory, mystery that will be revealed to you.

"You will shed many a tear as I show you My glory. As I reveal to you My glory, you will shed many a tear of intimacy and delight, that I am present to you in this time, in this way.

"When Moses came down from the Mount, his face was veiled because the glory on it was so strong. You are living in a time when that veil has been lifted. You shall see the Taboric glory that is on the face of My Son, as Peter, James, and John saw it.

"That Taboric glory is for you, My people, in this time of preparation for the Shekinah glory, the heavenly glory. You are called first to experience a revelation of the earthly glory. I will open your eyes to see it. I will open your heart to receive it. It is a gift from Me at this time for My people, for My bride.

"Say yes for yourself. Say yes for your family. Say yes for your community, for your church, for the churches of the world! Say yes for the bride that is so unready for a revelation of My glory! Say yes! That yes is heard in the heavenlies, even as Mary's yes was heard as she said, 'Be it done unto me according to Thy word.' She spoke it for the people, not just for herself. 'Let the Savior be born into this world.'"

Moses rested on his face for forty days and forty nights, after a revelation of the glory of God. I, too, in my Spirit say yes to resting on my face not just for forty days and forty nights, but for the rest of my life.

94

THE LORDSHIP OF JESUS

IT IS THE EARLY, early morning of August 29, that special day dedicated to the Lordship of Jesus, my Bridegroom. I am sitting in His awesome Presence. Seeing but not seeing. Hearing but not hearing. Listening for His voice.

"Franny, My Bride, I am here for you. I am here to thank you for being here for Me all these days. I have loved and enjoyed every precious moment of your stay here. Only eternity can tell the full story of all that happened, as you yielded your life on a new level to Mine.

"With Me a day is like a thousand years and a thousand years is like a day. Your being here has undergone a thousand years' gain of spiritual riches and glory. There is no going back. Only a going forward in your love story with the Father, Son, and Holy Spirit.

"Here, I have captured your heart on a level and to a degree that nothing can alter. Finally, you have surrendered your whole being to My bridal love for you. This can bring about changes in you greater than any other commitment; greater than when you accepted Me as your Lord and Savior; greater than when you accepted Me as your Baptizer in the Holy Spirit.

"Here in this place you have finally given to Me your all, your absolute all, in a Bridal Love relationship. By the power of My Spirit, I will teach you one day at a time what that means to have totally entered into a Bridal relationship with Divinity. You have readied yourself well for this grace. The rest is up to Me. I will not disappoint you nor will I fail you."

What does one do with a word like that in a place like this?

Say yes like the Maiden in Nazareth said yes. Say yes not just for yourself but for all who are called to walk this path and enter this intimate Bridal Love relationship.

That I might be sealed in the grace of the moment and favored with whatever other graces I needed, I asked Jesus to baptize me anew in His Holy Spirit with a Baptism of love that I might experience the love of my Bridegroom Jesus in whatever way He would choose to manifest it together with His glory. To be "two in one" in the heart of the Father was God's plan for me that day, to let go of my agendas and be open to Theirs.

Once again I played Connie Bence Boerner's *Love Songs from the Bridegroom.*

"Arise My beautiful bride and come with Me.

Arise, My lovely one, and come.

Arise My lovely one, the winter is past,

the rains are over and gone, and flowers appear on the earth.

In your heart a symphony is born.

Arise My beautiful one and come with Me."

Clothed in His righteousness, I received from the nail-scarred hands of my Bridegroom the gift of salvation for the bride that I would be called to pray for. There was nothing I could do, nothing I could add. It was all done. I spent a long time just being present to this truth, rejoicing in this mystery, knowing nothing could be greater. The most I could do was to stand tall in the promises, in the identity that my Bridegroom had given me, to be what He called me to be, to do what He called me to do, and to let go of everything else. The mystery needed to remain just that—mystery.

"Too late have I loved you. O beauty ancient but ever new" words from the Mass of St. Augustine whose feast day this was. How fitting that this was also the 51st anniversary of my leaving home to join the convent of the School Sisters of Notre Dame.

One more time I thanked Jesus for His faithfulness to me in those fifty-one years. I thanked Him for every grace, every blessing, every glory that had been poured out in my life.

I thanked Jesus for the grace of fidelity, "to hang in there tough" when it really was tough. I remembered the time His word to me was "Hang in there tough." You know what! He was right there with me hanging in there tough on His cross that I might know tough love.

I recalled the day a spiritual director responded to my need to understand with: "God must love you very much to give you such heavy crosses." My too-quick response was: "I wouldn't mind if He didn't love me quite so much."

God knows, I know, and a lot of people know that I have lived through some really tough times. I have seen "Ow, God" times! And I have seen "Wow, God" times! For a while it seemed to me that there were a lot more "Ow" than "Wow"! As I see it now, only eternity will tell how much the "Wow" outweighed the "Ow," how much the glory outweighed the suffering.

"For our light and momentary troubles are achieving for us an eternal glory that far outweighs them all" (2 Cor 4:17).

"You didn't choose Me, I chose you," Jesus reminded me. It is really true! Beyond every circumstance, it was Jesus who chose me to be in religious life, to do what I was called to do in a consecrated life of poverty, celibacy and obedience.

I remembered the day I renewed my vows with the words: "Jesus, I am Yours forever without reserve in gospel poverty." I heard Jesus say: "And I am yours in gospel riches!"

On this special day dedicated to my Bridegroom, I continued to renew my vows with: "I am Yours, Jesus, in consecrated celibacy."

He responded: "And I am yours in Bridal Love."

In awe I continued: "I am Yours in apostolic obedience."

"And I am Yours with power to live out that obedience. You are My obedient servant. You are My obedient bride."

There is no telling how many times each day I check to see if something is the desire of God's heart.

"More and more you are checking for the desires of
My heart before you launch out to undertake what
you would find yourself doing alone.
We are truly two in one in the Father, so it is only right
that I always be with My Bride.
It is only right that as you move throughout your day
you can say, 'We decide, We enjoy.
We serve, We rejoice.
We pause to pray.
For We are truly two in one, Bride and Bridegroom, in
the heart of the Father."

Between the prophetic words from *We, the Bride* and the paraphrased Scripture, Jesus gave me rich, rich fare for the day.

"I love you, My Bride, with a perfect love that cares
for all the worry within you.
I do not like seeing you anxious.
In My time I will take care of all that is worry or
anxiety within you.
You can trust your God.

If I have been a faithful God in the past
a provider God in the past
a Bridegroom God in the past
you will find Me a thousand times more in your
todays and in your tomorrows.
You have married a faithful God. The best is yet to be!
Ask for yourself and for others those graces and
blessings that I have put close to your heart.
This is a Divine romance you are in.
All the resources of heaven and earth are at My
disposal to court you as My Bride.
Be prepared for surprises!"

"Think of the love that the Father has lavished on you by letting you be called God's children. That is what you are, but what we are to be in the future, as the bride of Jesus, has not yet been revealed. All we know is that when it is revealed, we shall all be like our Bridegroom because we shall see Him as He really is" (1 Jn 3:1-3, my paraphrase).

The entrance antiphon for today's Mass was from Sirach 15:5: "The Lord opened His mouth in the assembly and filled Him with the Spirit of wisdom and understanding and clothed Him in a robe of glory." God's promise was to fill me with the spirit of wisdom and understanding, not just myself but you, and to clothe you with a robe of glory!

As the sun was setting, God set on my heart this word for you:

"I speak to you today a word of love.
I have never loved you so much.
I have never desired your response to My love so
much.
This is a journey of love,
in which your love can only grow stronger, as you
realize how strong My love is for you,
how constant My love is for you,
how unchanging My love is for you.
It is like the waves of a mighty ocean, the waves never
cease.
The water constantly comes and goes.
The water constantly pours forth in waves of
fullness.
That's the way My love is constantly flowing over

your life like waves of the ocean,
    cleansing you, healing you, freeing you,
    empowering you, enabling you to do all
    that I call you to do.
I am pleased, very pleased,
    when you dedicate a special day like today
    just to Me that I may speak to you.
It is not that the Father isn't here,
    but you are being called to a special day
    centered upon My love for you
    as Bridegroom for the bride.
Together we stand in the heart of the Father
    but you are to listen to Me today,
    to listen to the words that I speak,
    to follow the directions that I give,
    to keep your eyes on Me,
    to keep your heart open to My direction!
There are things you do not need to do.
    Thoughts you do not need to think.
You are a new person, a new creation.
    You stand clothed in My righteousness.
    Every other kind of righteousness can go.
You have fallen short of the glory of God in many
    ways in the past.
But you will fall short less and less as you realize that
    all your righteousness is as filthy rags.
There is nothing you can do to earn My love.
It is yours free. You don't earn it. You receive it.
You say yes to it and you allow it to bathe you,
    to clothe you, to fill you,
    to imbue you with power from on high,
    to clothe you in My glory.
Yes, I am pleased with how you have arranged and
    followed through this day.
I thank you for the special bouquet of bridal blossoms
    shaken from the tree last night, that you picked up
    on your walk.
They rest on the table as a symbol of your love for Me
    and My love for you.

I thank you for the desire you have to appreciate the
beauty that is all around you.
Know that the beauty that is all around you is nothing
compared to the beauty that is in you.
My life in you.
My love in you.
My beauty in you is growing day by day
minute by minute, task by task,
Scripture by Scripture, prayer by prayer.
I am here for you, My bride!
For whatever you need, I am here.
I am with you."

"We are God's children now; what we shall later be has not yet come to light. We know that when it comes to light we shall be like him for we shall see him as he is" (1 Jn 3:2).

That word like a golden thread and a trumpet blast ran through this whole day dedicated to Jesus. We shall all be like Him for we shall see Him as He really is soon and very soon.

"My darling bride, there is no standing still for you.
We are in the chariot race together!
I see you with winged feet and a winged heart.
Come, My darling Bride, we shall cut new records in
the race to love and to be loved!
One lifetime can hardly be enough to experience the
love of your Beloved.
That is what eternity is all about."

95

THE HOLY SPIRIT

IT IS THE VIGIL of August 30, the day dedicated to the Holy Spirit.
God's word came forth in power before my night's rest:
"On this day dedicated to the outpouring of My Holy
Spirit,
I bring forth from deep within you wells of Living
Water.
I cleanse you on levels deeper than you have ever
been cleansed.
I empower you on levels beyond anything that you
have known.
For you have cried out to Me for a deeper release of
My Holy Spirit.
You have cried out for a deeper relationship with My
Holy Spirit.
This night, I say to you, I will pour forth My Holy Spirit
beyond anything you can comprehend in your
human spirit or dream up in your faith imagination.
I, Jesus, your baptizer in the Holy Spirit,
have indeed immersed you in My Holy Spirit,
My Light, My Life, My Love, My Power.
I have immersed your mind in My Spirit,
your understanding in My Spirit,
every part of your spiritual being has been immersed
in My Holy Spirit.
The Spirit of the Lord that is upon you is not intended
for just one day.
It is intended to stay!
'There stands one in your midst Who will baptize you
[continually] in the Holy Spirit and in fire' (Mt 3:11).
I give to you this night a mighty resting in the power
of My Holy Spirit.
Even as you are resting I shall be in eternal activity
for I see nothing in you to block My power,
nothing to block My light, nothing to block My love.

This entire night I bathe you, clothe you,
   empower you with My Spirit.
It was a night like no other night on the Divine Potter's
   Wheel!"

"All of us, gazing on the Lord's glory with unveiled faces,
are being transformed from glory to glory into His very image by
the Lord who is the Spirit" (2 Cor 3:18) (NAB).

Before I could begin to program my day, Jesus had a word
for me:

"Frannie, My bride, throughout this whole journey
   by the power of the Holy Spirit
   you have stood together in faith with Me
   in the heart of the Father.
You have stood owning your sinfulness
   and allowed Me in ways you never dreamed of
   to clothe you in My righteousness.
Today as My bride you stand together with Me
   in the heart of the Father.
   Clothed in a glory you cannot see but it is real!
   Clothed in a glory that you would only mar or limit
   if you could see it.
All the Bride that is triumphant sees you.
   All the Heavenly Court sees you!
   All the angels that you have so honored
   and asked again and again to intercede for you see
   you!
They applaud what God has done in you.
They applaud how God has used you for a book
   that He will give page by page, line by line, thought
   by thought.
As the book moves, people will move from a place of
   apprehension, hopelessness, even complacency,
   to a place of realization that their God is moving in
   power!
What your God has promised is coming to fulfillment!
Your God is preparing His people with new gifts,
   cleansing them with the Precious Blood,
   empowering them with His Holy Word.
Your God is bringing them to an awareness that He is
   coming soon.

And very soon!
This is mystery that no one will ever fully understand
or be able to share in a book, an article, or a song.
No one will ever be able to fully preach it from a pulpit
or teach it at a prayer meeting.
It is *mystery!* Your God is at work!
Nothing can halt the Hand of your God!"
More and more in ways that only the Spirit can move and lead us, we will be called to share the glory in our lives. Only the Spirit can move us beyond our struggle and our pain, beyond our confusion and our defeat, to a place where we can celebrate the victory, the power, and the glory we have in our God.

When I get to eternal glory I will be so glad to know that again and again I have called on Michael, Gabriel, Raphael and all the choirs of angels to be there to fight the good fight, not just for me but for all peoples! When Gabriel blows his trumpet, I will be delighted to know that I have often prayed, "Blow it Gabriel! Blow that trumpet! Hail the coming of the King of Kings!"

My anointing is upon you this day.
Even as My anointing so is My glory upon you.
My glory floods your mind, your heart, your spirit.
My glory floods your spirit with My Holy Spirit.
This day I say to you even as you say to Me,
Holy, holy, holy! Holy are you!
Holy are you, My children, for you are full of My
glory.
Heaven and earth is full of My glory,
but it is nothing compared to the glory
that I pour forth upon you as you recognize and
admit My life in your life!
This day I would have you bathe in My glory,
bask in My glory, be redeemed anew with My glory,
for I, the Lord your God, am a God of glory.
I bring you this day to a new experience
of who you are and Who I AM.
I fill you this day, with a new measure of glory.
I am transforming you from glory to glory.
I am lifting you up above all that is circumstance
in your life, above all that is drab, dull and earthy.
I am lifting you up so that you might experience this day

a kiss of My glory.
As you look about you, you see a world full of glory,
    full of sunshine, the beauty of nature,
    waving palms, brilliant flowers,
    smiles on the faces of My people.
All this is earthly glory.
Look above you to the world beyond you,
    the world that is invisible, the world where I live in
    glory.
See the promise of a future glory.
Experience today in the very depths of your being
    the promise of a future glory that will not fade,
    that will not pass away.
I have prepared for you from all eternity a share in My
    glory,
    the glory of My eternal existence,
    the glory that eye has not seen nor ear heard,
    nor has it entered into the heart of anyone
    to dream what I have prepared for those who love Me.
Dream dreams, My beautiful people.
'In the latter days I will pour out My Spirit on all flesh
    and your old men will dream dreams' (Jl 3:1).
Dream dreams for a future full of glory,
    a future full of love,
    a future full of hope.
How often have I spoken to you about delighting in Me
    so that I might delight in you.
Delight this day in the glory that is around you,
    the glory that is in the beauty of nature,
    the glory that is in the beauty of your children,
    the glory that is in your family, your church,
    your community!
Delight in the glory of who you are
    and who I have made you!
    You are a child of glory!
        My glory is deep within you.
        My glory is high above you.
        My glory is all around you.
    You are a child of glory! My glory is in you.
I have been a God of glory for Abraham, Isaac, Jacob,

Moses, Judith, Esther, David, Mary, the Mother of
Jesus, Peter, James, and John.
Although My glory was hidden, I have been a God of
glory as I walked the face of the earth.
I who ascended into glory, will come again in glory,
receive you into glory!
You, My people. You who are reading this,
I will receive you into a glory for all eternity.
This day allow yourself to dream dreams.
Allow yourself to be caught up into that eternal reality.
For this is reality beyond the floor on which you stand,
the air you now breathe, the eyes you now see with,
the ears you now hear with.
Beyond all that your senses experience in the now,
know the eternal glory is for you!
Dream dreams and I, your God, will be with you
to put those dreams upon your conscious and your
subconscious.
Blessed are those who dare to dream dreams
and are willing to pay the price to have them come
true.
Reach out today and discover for yourself anew
that I am a God of glory.
I have been a God of glory from all eternity.
I have manifested My glory to the great patriarchs,
prophets and saints of old.
I have dwelt among them in a cloud of glory by day
and a pillar of fire by night.
I AM the same God who dwells among you today,
in your churches, in your prayer meetings and
worship gatherings.
I AM pouring forth My glory into your very being.
I AM hovering over you with a mantle
of protection, peace, love, glory.
In no way can the enemy draw near to you.
In no way can the enemy destroy you.
For you are Mine and I am yours!"

I asked myself one more time can this really be true? Could
a God of such dimensions of glory care about me, redeem me and

promise eternal salvation and glory to such a one as me? I have merited nothing of this glory.

"All is gift!"

How can I believe for a future full of glory except that my God has promised it. God's promises will not fail. "For truly I tell you, until heaven and earth pass away, not one letter, not one stroke of a letter, will pass from the law until all is accomplished" (Mt 5:18) (AIV).

Only my unbelief can bring His promises to naught in my life. If I choose other gods or a fading temporal glory in exchange for eternal glory, how foolish can I get?

God of glory, deal with my foolishness. You are so big! I am so little!

"The whole world before you is like a speck that tips the scales, and like a drop of morning dew that falls on the ground" (Wis 11:22) (NRS).

This day and for the rest of my life, I yield to You my whole being, like a grain of sand that tips the scales, a drop of morning

Published by Resurrection Press

A Rachel Rosary *Larry Kupferman*	$3.95
Catholic Is Wonderful *Mitch Finley*	$4.95
Common Bushes *Kieran Kay*	$8.95
Christian Marriage *John & Therese Boucher*	$3.95
Come, Celebrate Jesus! *Francis X. Gaeta*	$4.95
From Holy Hour to Happy Hour *Francis X. Gaeta*	$7.95
Healing through the Mass *Robert DeGrandis, SSJ*	$7.95
Healing the Wounds of Emotional Abuse *Nancy Benvenga*	$6.95
Healing Your Grief *Ruthann Williams, OP*	$7.95
Living Each Day by the Power of Faith *Barbara Ryan*	$8.95
Inwords *Mary Kraemer, OSF*	$4.50
The Healing of the Religious Life *Faricy/Blackborow*	$6.95
The Joy of Being a Catechist *Gloria Durka*	$4.50
The Joy of Being a Eucharistic Minister *Mitch Finley*	$4.95
Transformed by Love *Margaret Magdalen, CSMV*	$5.95
RVC Liturgical Series: The Liturgy of the Hours	$3.95
The Lector's Ministry	$3.95
Behold the Man *Judy Marley, SFO*	$4.50
Lights in the Darkness *Ave Clark, O.P.*	$8.95
Loving Yourself for God's Sake *Adolfo Quezada*	$5.95
Practicing the Prayer of Presence *van Kaam/Muto*	$7.95
5-Minute Miracles *Linda Schubert*	$3.95
Nothing but Love *Robert Lauder*	$3.95
Healthy and Holy under Stress *van Kaam/Muto*	$3.95
Season of New Beginnings *Mitch Finley*	$4.50
Season of Promises *Mitch Finley*	$4.50
Soup Pot *Ethel Pochocki*	$8.95
Stay with Us *John Mullin, SJ*	$3.95
Surprising Mary *Mitch Finley*	$7.95
What He Did for Love *Francis X. Gaeta*	$4.95

For a free catalog call 1-800-892-6657